W9-AWE-172

On
Women and
Leadership

HBR's 10 Must Reads series is the definitive collection of ideas and best practices for aspiring and experienced leaders alike. These books offer essential reading selected from the pages of *Harvard Business Review* on topics critical to the success of every manager.

Titles include:

HBR's 10 Must Reads 2015
HBR's 10 Must Reads 2016
HBR's 10 Must Reads 2017
HBR's 10 Must Reads 2018
HBR's 10 Must Reads 2019
HBR's 10 Must Reads for New Managers
HBR's 10 Must Reads on Change Management
HBR's 10 Must Reads on Collaboration
HBR's 10 Must Reads on Communication
HBR's 10 Must Reads on Emotional Intelligence
HBR's 10 Must Reads on Entrepreneurship and Startups
HBR's 10 Must Reads on Innovation
HBR's 10 Must Reads on Leadership
HBR's 10 Must Reads on Leadership for Healthcare
HBR's 10 Must Reads on Leadership Lessons from Sports
HBR's 10 Must Reads on Making Smart Decisions
HBR's 10 Must Reads on Managing Across Cultures
HBR's 10 Must Reads on Managing People
HBR's 10 Must Reads on Managing Yourself
HBR's 10 Must Reads on Mental Toughness
HBR's 10 Must Reads on Sales
HBR's 10 Must Reads on Strategic Marketing
HBR's 10 Must Reads on Strategy
HBR's 10 Must Reads on Strategy for Healthcare
HBR's 10 Must Reads on Teams
HBR's 10 Must Reads: The Essentials

On
Women and
Leadership

HARVARD BUSINESS REVIEW PRESS
Boston, Massachusetts

HBR Press Quantity Sales Discounts

Harvard Business Review Press titles are available at significant quantity discounts when purchased in bulk for client gifts, sales promotions, and premiums. Special editions, including books with corporate logos, customized covers, and letters from the company or CEO printed in the front matter, as well as excerpts of existing books, can also be created in large quantities for special needs.

For details and discount information for both print and ebook formats, contact booksales@harvardbusiness.org, tel. 800-988-0886, or www.hbr.org/bulksales.

The web addresses referenced in this book were live and correct at the time of the book's publication but may be subject to change.

Cataloging-in-publication data is forthcoming.

The paper used in this publication meets the requirements of the American National Standard for Permanence of Paper for Publications and Documents in Libraries and Archives Z39.48-1992.

ISBN: 9781633696723
eISBN: 9781633696730

Contents

Women and the Labyrinth of Leadership   1
by Alice H. Eagly and Linda L. Carli

Do Women Lack Ambition?   21
by Anna Fels

Women Rising: The Unseen Barriers   39
by Herminia Ibarra, Robin Ely, and Deborah Kolb

Women and the Vision Thing   51
by Herminia Ibarra and Otilia Obodaru

The Power of Talk: Who Gets Heard and Why   67
by Deborah Tannen

The Memo Every Woman Keeps in Her Desk   91
by Kathleen Reardon

Why Diversity Programs Fail   103
by Frank Dobbin and Alexandra Kalev

Now What?   119
by Joan C. Williams and Suzanne Lebsock

The Battle for Female Talent in Emerging Markets   145
by Sylvia Ann Hewlett and Ripa Rashid

Off-Ramps and On-Ramps: Keeping Talented Women on the Road to Success   157
by Sylvia Ann Hewlett and Carolyn Buck Luce

BONUS
Sheryl Sandberg: The HBR Interview   179
An interview with Sheryl Sandberg by Adi Ignatius

About the Contributors   193
Index   197

On
**Women and
Leadership**

Women and the Labyrinth of Leadership

by Alice H. Eagly and Linda L. Carli

IF ONE HAS MISDIAGNOSED A PROBLEM, then one is unlikely to pre-scribe an effective cure. This is the situation regarding the scarcity of women in top leadership. Because people with the best of intentions have misread the symptoms, the solutions that managers are invest-ing in are not making enough of a difference.

That there is a problem is not in doubt. Despite years of progress by women in the workforce (they now occupy more than 40% of all managerial positions in the United States), within the C-suite they remain as rare as hens' teeth. Consider the most highly paid execu-tives of *Fortune* 500 companies—those with titles such as chairman, president, chief executive officer, and chief operating officer. Of this group, only 6% are women. Most notably, only 2% of the CEOs are women, and only 15% of the seats on the boards of directors are held by women. The situation is not much different in other indus-trialized countries. In the 50 largest publicly traded corporations in each nation of the European Union, women make up, on average, 11% of the top executives and 4% of the CEOs and heads of boards. Just seven companies, or 1%, of *Fortune* magazine's Global 500 have female CEOs. What is to blame for the pronounced lack of women in positions of power and authority?

In 1986 the *Wall Street Journal*'s Carol Hymowitz and Timothy Schellhardt gave the world an answer: "Even those few women who rose steadily through the ranks eventually crashed into an invisible barrier. The executive suite seemed within their grasp, but they just couldn't break through the glass ceiling." The metaphor, driven home by the article's accompanying illustration, resonated; it captured the frustration of a goal within sight but somehow unattainable. To be sure, there was a time when the barriers were absolute. Even within the career spans of 1980s-era executives, access to top posts had been explicitly denied. Consider comments made by President Richard Nixon, recorded on White House audiotapes and made public through the Freedom of Information Act. When explaining why he would not appoint a woman to the U.S. Supreme Court, Nixon said, "I don't think a woman should be in any government job whatsoever. . .mainly because they are erratic. And emotional. Men are erratic and emotional, too, but the point is a woman is more likely to be." In a culture where such opinions were widely held, women had virtually no chance of attaining influential leadership roles.

Times have changed, however, and the glass ceiling metaphor is now more wrong than right. For one thing, it describes an absolute barrier at a specific high level in organizations. The fact that there have been female chief executives, university presidents, state governors, and presidents of nations gives the lie to that charge. At the same time, the metaphor implies that women and men have equal access to entry- and midlevel positions. They do not. The image of a transparent obstruction also suggests that women are being misled about their opportunities, because the impediment is not easy for them to see from a distance. But some impediments are not subtle. Worst of all, by depicting a single, unvarying obstacle, the glass ceiling fails to incorporate the complexity and variety of challenges that women can face in their leadership journeys. In truth, women are not turned away only as they reach the penultimate stage of a distinguished career. They disappear in various numbers at many points leading up to that stage.

Metaphors matter because they are part of the storytelling that can compel change. Believing in the existence of a glass ceiling, people emphasize certain kinds of interventions: top-to-top networking,

Idea in Brief

Women occupy 40% of all managerial positions in the United States. But only 6% of the *Fortune* 500's top executives are female. And just 2% of those firms have women CEOs.

We've long blamed such numbers on the "glass ceiling," the notion that women successfully climb the corporate hierarchy until they're blocked just below the summit. But the problem stems from discrimination operating at all ranks, not just the top, say Eagly and Carli.

Therefore, to move more women into your company's executive suite, you must attack all barriers to advancement simultaneously. For example, prepare women for line management with demanding assignments. Use objective criteria to measure performance. And give working mothers additional time to prove themselves worthy of promotion.

Women's leadership style—characterized by innovating, building trust and empowering followers—is ideally suited to today's business challenges. Tackle the obstacles to women's progress, and you'll increase your firm's competitive prowess.

mentoring to increase board memberships, requirements for diverse candidates in high-profile succession horse races, litigation aimed at punishing discrimination in the C-suite. None of these is counterproductive; all have a role to play. The danger arises when they draw attention and resources away from other kinds of interventions that might attack the problem more potently. If we want to make better progress, it's time to rename the challenge.

Walls All Around

A better metaphor for what confronts women in their professional endeavors is the labyrinth. It's an image with a long and varied history in ancient Greece, India, Nepal, native North and South America, medieval Europe, and elsewhere. As a contemporary symbol, it conveys the idea of a complex journey toward a goal worth striving for. Passage through a labyrinth is not simple or direct, but requires persistence, awareness of one's progress, and a careful analysis of the puzzles that lie ahead. It is this meaning that we intend to convey. For women who aspire to top leadership, routes exist but

Idea in Practice

Eagly and Carli recommend these strategies for increasing the number of women in top positions in your firm:

Understand the Career Barriers Women Encounter

Extensive academic and government research studies identify these obstacles:

- **Prejudice:** Men are promoted more quickly than women with equivalent qualifications, even in traditionally female settings such as nursing and education.

- **Resistance to women's leadership:** People view successful female managers as more deceitful, pushy, selfish, and abrasive than successful male managers.

- **Leadership style issues:** Many female leaders struggle to reconcile qualities people prefer in women (compassion for others) with qualities people think leaders need to succeed (assertion and control).

- **Family demands:** Women are still the ones who interrupt their careers to handle work/family trade-offs. Overloaded, they lack time to engage in the social networking essential to advancement.

Intervene on Multiple Fronts

Because of the interconnectedness of obstacles women face, companies that want more women leaders need to apply a variety of tactics simultaneously:

- Evaluate and reward women's productivity by objective results, not by "number of hours at work."

- Make performance-evaluation criteria explicit, and design evaluation processes to limit the influence of evaluators' biases.

- Instead of relying on informal social networks and referrals

are full of twists and turns, both unexpected and expected. Because all labyrinths have a viable route to the center, it is understood that goals are attainable. The metaphor acknowledges obstacles but is not ultimately discouraging.

If we can understand the various barriers that make up this labyrinth, and how some women find their way around them, we can work more effectively to improve the situation. What are the obstructions that women run up against? Let's explore them in turn.

to fill positions, use open-recruitment tools such as advertising and employment agencies.

- Avoid having a sole female member on any team. Outnumbered, women tend to be ignored by men.

- Encourage well-placed, widely esteemed individuals to mentor women.

- Ensure a critical mass of women in executive positions to head off problems that come with tokenism. Women's identities as women will become less salient to colleagues than their individual competencies.

- Give women demanding developmental job experiences to train them for leadership positions.

- Establish family-friendly HR practices (including flextime, job sharing, and telecommuting). You'll help women stay in their jobs while rearing children, allow them to build social capital, and enable them eventually to compete for higher positions. Encourage men to participate in family-friendly benefits, too (for example, by providing paternity leave). When only women participate, their careers suffer because companies expect them to be off the job while exercising those options.

- Give employees with significant parental responsibilities more time to show they're qualified for promotion. Parents may need a year or two more than childless professionals.

- Establish alumni programs for women who need to step away from the workforce. Then tap their expertise to show that returning is possible. Consulting giant Booz Allen, for example, sees its alumni as a source of subcontractors.

Vestiges of prejudice

It is a well-established fact that men as a group still have the benefit of higher wages and faster promotions. In the United States in 2005, for example, women employed full-time earned 81 cents for every dollar that men earned. Is this true because of discrimination or simply because, with fewer family demands placed on them and longer careers on average, men are able to gain superior qualifications? Literally hundreds of correlational studies by economists and sociologists have attempted to find the answer.

One of the most comprehensive of these studies was conducted by the U.S. Government Accountability Office. The study was based on survey data from 1983 through 2000 from a representative sample of Americans. Because the same people responded to the survey repeatedly over the years, the study provided accurate estimates of past work experience, which is important for explaining later wages.

The GAO researchers tested whether individuals' total wages could be predicted by sex and other characteristics. They included part-time and full-time employees in the surveys and took into account all the factors that they could estimate and that might affect earnings, such as education and work experience. Without controls for these variables, the data showed that women earned about 44% less than men, averaged over the entire period from 1983 to 2000. With these controls in place, the gap was only about half as large, but still substantial. The control factors that reduced the wage gap most were the different employment patterns of men and women: Men undertook more hours of paid labor per year than women and had more years of job experience.

Although most variables affected the wages of men and women similarly, there were exceptions. Marriage and parenthood, for instance, were associated with higher wages for men but not for women. In contrast, other characteristics, especially years of education, had a more positive effect on women's wages than on men's. Even after adjusting wages for all of the ways men and women differ, the GAO study, like similar studies, showed that women's wages remained lower than men's. The unexplained gender gap is consistent with the presence of wage discrimination.

Similar methods have been applied to the question of whether discrimination affects promotions. Evidently it does. Promotions come more slowly for women than for men with equivalent qualifications. One illustrative national study followed workers from 1980 to 1992 and found that white men were more likely to attain managerial positions than white women, black men, and black women. Controlling for other characteristics, such as education and hours worked per year, the study showed that white men were ahead of the other groups when entering the labor market and that their advantage in attaining managerial positions grew throughout their careers. Other research has underscored these findings. Even in culturally feminine settings such as nursing, librarianship, elementary education, and social work (all specifically studied by sociologist Christine Williams), men ascend to supervisory and administrative positions more quickly than women.

The findings of correlational studies are supported by experimental research, in which subjects are asked to evaluate hypothetical individuals as managers or job candidates, and all characteristics of these individuals are held constant except for their sex. Such efforts continue the tradition of the Goldberg paradigm, named for a 1968 experiment by Philip Goldberg. His simple, elegant study had student participants evaluate written essays that were identical except for the attached male or female name. The students were unaware that other students had received identical material ascribed to a writer of the other sex. This initial experiment demonstrated an overall gender bias: Women received lower evaluations unless the essay was on a feminine topic. Some 40 years later, unfortunately, experiments continue to reveal the same kind of bias in work settings. Men are advantaged over equivalent women as candidates for jobs traditionally held by men as well as for more gender-integrated jobs. Similarly, male leaders receive somewhat more favorable evaluations than equivalent female leaders, especially in roles usually occupied by men.

Interestingly, however, there is little evidence from either the correlational or the experimental studies that the odds are stacked higher against women with each step up the ladder—that is, that women's promotions become progressively less likely than men's at higher levels within organizations. Instead, a general bias against women appears to operate with approximately equal strength at all levels. The scarcity of female corporate officers is the sum of discrimination that has operated at all ranks, not evidence of a particular obstacle to advancement as women approach the top. The problem, in other words, is not a glass ceiling.

Resistance to women's leadership

What's behind the discrimination we've been describing? Essentially, a set of widely shared conscious and unconscious mental associations about women, men, and leaders. Study after study has affirmed that people associate women and men with different traits and link men with more of the traits that connote leadership. Kim Campbell, who briefly served as the prime minister of Canada in 1993, described the tension that results:

I don't have a traditionally female way of speaking. . . . I'm quite assertive. If I didn't speak the way I do, I wouldn't have been seen as a leader. But my way of speaking may have grated on people who were not used to hearing it from a woman. It was the right way for a leader to speak, but it wasn't the right way for a woman to speak. It goes against type.

In the language of psychologists, the clash is between two sets of associations: communal and agentic. Women are associated with communal qualities, which convey a concern for the compassionate treatment of others. They include being especially affectionate, helpful, friendly, kind, and sympathetic, as well as interpersonally sensitive, gentle, and soft-spoken. In contrast, men are associated with agentic qualities, which convey assertion and control. They include being especially aggressive, ambitious, dominant, self-confident, and forceful, as well as self-reliant and individualistic. The agentic traits are also associated in most people's minds with effective leadership—perhaps because a long history of male domination of leadership roles has made it difficult to separate the leader associations from the male associations.

As a result, women leaders find themselves in a double bind. If they are highly communal, they may be criticized for not being agentic enough. But if they are highly agentic, they may be criticized for lacking communion. Either way, they may leave the impression that they don't have "the right stuff" for powerful jobs.

Given this double bind, it is hardly surprising that people are more resistant to women's influence than to men's. For example, in meetings at a global retail company, people responded more favorably to men's overt attempts at influence than to women's. In the words of one of this company's female executives, "People often had to speak up to defend their turf, but when women did so, they were vilified. They were labeled 'control freaks'; men acting the same way were called 'passionate.'"

Studies have gauged reactions to men and women engaging in various types of dominant behavior. The findings are quite consistent. Nonverbal dominance, such as staring at others while speaking to them or pointing at people, is a more damaging behavior for women than for men. Verbally intimidating others can undermine a woman's influence, and assertive behavior can reduce her chances of getting a job or advancing in her career. Simply disagreeing can sometimes get women into trouble. Men who disagree or otherwise act dominant get away with it more often than women do.

Self-promotion is similarly risky for women. Although it can convey status and competence, it is not at all communal. So while men can use bluster to get themselves noticed, modesty is expected even of highly accomplished women. Linguistics professor Deborah Tannen tells a story from her experience: "This [need for modesty] was evident, for example, at a faculty meeting devoted to promotions, at which a woman professor's success was described: She was extremely well published and well known in the field. A man commented with approval, 'She wears it well.' In other words, she was praised for not acting as successful as she was."

Another way the double bind penalizes women is by denying them the full benefits of being warm and considerate. Because people expect it of women, nice behavior that seems noteworthy in men seems unimpressive in women. For example, in one study, helpful men reaped a lot of approval, but helpful women did not. Likewise, men got away with being unhelpful, but women did not. A different study found that male employees received more promotions when they reported higher levels of helpfulness to coworkers. But female employees' promotions were not related to such altruism.

While one might suppose that men would have a double bind of their own, they in fact have more freedom. Several experiments and organizational studies have assessed reactions to behavior that is warm and friendly versus dominant and assertive. The findings show that men can communicate in a warm or a dominant manner, with no penalty either way. People like men equally well and are equally influenced by them regardless of their warmth.

It all amounts to a clash of assumptions when the average person confronts a woman in management. Perhaps this is why respondents in one study characterized the group "successful female managers" as more deceitful, pushy, selfish, and abrasive than "successful male managers." In the absence of any evidence to the contrary, people suspect that such highly effective women must not be very likable or nice.

Issues of leadership style

In response to the challenges presented by the double bind, female leaders often struggle to cultivate an appropriate and effective leadership style—one that reconciles the communal qualities people prefer in women with the agentic qualities people think leaders need to succeed. Here, for instance, is how Marietta Nien-hwa Cheng described her transition to the role of symphony conductor:

> I used to speak more softly, with a higher pitch. Sometimes my vocal cadences went up instead of down. I realized that these mannerisms lack the sense of authority. I strengthened my voice. The pitch has dropped. . . . I have stopped trying to be everyone's friend. Leadership is not synonymous with socializing.

It's difficult to pull off such a transformation while maintaining a sense of authenticity as a leader. Sometimes the whole effort can backfire. In the words of another female leader, "I think that there is a real penalty for a woman who behaves like a man. The men don't like her and the women don't either." Women leaders worry a lot about these things, complicating the labyrinth that they negotiate. For example, Catalyst's study of *Fortune* 1000 female executives found that 96% of them rated as critical or fairly important that they develop "a style with which male managers are comfortable."

Does a distinct "female" leadership style exist? There seems to be a popular consensus that it does. Consider, for example, journalist Michael Sokolove's profile of Mike Krzyzewski, head coach

Is It Only a Question of Time?

IT IS A COMMON PERCEPTION that women will steadily gain greater access to leadership roles, including elite positions. For example, university students who are queried about the future power of men and women say that women's power will increase. Polls have shown that most Americans expect a woman to be elected president or vice president within their lifetimes. Both groups are extrapolating women's recent gains into the future, as if our society were on a continuous march toward gender equality.

But social change does not proceed without struggle and conflict. As women gain greater equality, a portion of people react against it. They long for traditional roles. In fact, signs of a pause in progress toward gender equality have appeared on many fronts. A review of longitudinal studies reveals several areas in which a sharp upward trend in the 1970s and 1980s has been followed by a slowing and flattening in recent years (for instance, in the percentage of managers who are women). The pause is also evident in some attitudinal data—like the percentage of people who approve of female bosses and who believe that women are at least as well suited as men for politics.

Social scientists have proposed various theories to explain this pause. Some, such as social psychologist Cecilia Ridgeway, believe that social change is activating "people's deep seated interests in maintaining clear cultural understandings of gender difference." Others believe progress has reached its limit given the continuing organization of family life by gender, coupled with employer policies that favor those who are not hampered by primary responsibility for child rearing.

It may simply be that women are collectively catching their breath before pressing for more change. In the past century, feminist activism arose when women came to view themselves as collectively subjected to illegitimate and unfair treatment. But recent polls show less conviction about the presence of discrimination, and feminism does not have the cultural relevance it once had. The lessening of activism on behalf of all women puts pressure on each woman to find her own way.

---

of the highly successful Duke University men's basketball team. As Sokolove put it, "So what is the secret to Krzyzewski's success? For starters, he coaches the way a woman would. Really." Sokolove proceeded to describe Krzyzewski's mentoring, interpersonally sensitive, and highly effective coaching style.

More scientifically, a recent meta-analysis integrated the results of 45 studies addressing the question. To compare leadership skills, the researchers adopted a framework introduced by leadership scholar James MacGregor Burns that distinguishes between transformational leadership and transactional leadership. Transformational leaders establish themselves as role models by gaining followers' trust and confidence. They state future goals, develop plans to achieve those goals, and innovate, even when their organizations are generally successful. Such leaders mentor and empower followers, encouraging them to develop their full potential and thus to contribute more effectively to their organizations. By contrast, transactional leaders establish give-and-take relationships that appeal to subordinates' self-interest. Such leaders manage in the conventional manner of clarifying subordinates' responsibilities, rewarding them for meeting objectives, and correcting them for failing to meet objectives. Although transformational and transactional leadership styles are different, most leaders adopt at least some behaviors of both types. The researchers also allowed for a third category, called the laissez-faire style—a sort of nonleadership that concerns itself with none of the above, despite rank authority.

The meta-analysis found that, in general, female leaders were somewhat more transformational than male leaders, especially when it came to giving support and encouragement to subordinates. They also engaged in more of the rewarding behaviors that are one aspect of transactional leadership. Meanwhile, men exceeded women on the aspects of transactional leadership involving corrective and disciplinary actions that are either active (timely) or passive (belated). Men were also more likely than women to be laissez-faire leaders, who take little responsibility for managing. These findings add up to a startling conclusion, given that most leadership research has found the transformational style (along with the rewards and positive incentives associated with the transactional style) to be more suited to leading the modern organization. The research tells us not only that men and women do have somewhat different leadership styles, but also that women's approaches are the more generally effective—while men's often are only somewhat effective or actually hinder effectiveness.

Another part of this picture, based on a separate meta-analysis, is that women adopt a more participative and collaborative style than men typically favor. The reason for this difference is unlikely to be genetic. Rather, it may be that collaboration can get results without seeming particularly masculine. As women navigate their way through the double bind, they seek ways to project authority without relying on the autocratic behaviors that people find so jarring in women. A viable path is to bring others into decision making and to lead as an encouraging teacher and positive role model. (However, if there is not a critical mass of other women to affirm the legitimacy of a participative style, female leaders usually conform to whatever style is typical of the men—and that is sometimes autocratic.)

Demands of family life

For many women, the most fateful turns in the labyrinth are the ones taken under pressure of family responsibilities. Women continue to be the ones who interrupt their careers, take more days off, and work part-time. As a result, they have fewer years of job experience and fewer hours of employment per year, which slows their career progress and reduces their earnings.

In one study of Chicago lawyers, researchers sought to understand why women were much less likely than men to hold the leadership positions in large law firms—the positions that are most highly paid and that confer (arguably) the highest prestige. They found that women were no less likely than men to begin their careers at such firms but were more likely to leave them for positions in the public sector or corporate positions. The reasons for their departures were concentrated in work/family trade-offs. Among the relatively few women who did become partner in a firm, 60% had no children, and the minority who had children generally had delayed childbearing until attaining partner status.

There is no question that, while men increasingly share housework and child rearing, the bulk of domestic work still falls on women's shoulders. We know this from time-diary studies, in which people record what they are doing during each hour of a 24-hour day. So, for example, in the United States married women devoted

19 hours per week on average to housework in 2005, while married men contributed 11 hours. That's a huge improvement over 1965 numbers, when women spent a whopping 34 hours per week to men's five, but it is still a major inequity. And the situation looks worse when child care hours are added.

Although it is common knowledge that mothers provide more child care than fathers, few people realize that mothers provide more than they did in earlier generations—despite the fact that fathers are putting in a lot more time than in the past. National studies have compared mothers and fathers on the amount of their primary child care, which consists of close interaction not combined with housekeeping or other activities. Married mothers increased their hours per week from 10.6 in 1965 to 12.9 in 2000, and married fathers increased theirs from 2.6 to 6.5. Thus, though husbands have taken on more domestic work, the work/family conflict has not eased for women; the gain has been offset by escalating pressures for intensive parenting and the increasing time demands of most high-level careers.

Even women who have found a way to relieve pressures from the home front by sharing child care with husbands, other family members, or paid workers may not enjoy the full workplace benefit of having done so. Decision makers often assume that mothers have domestic responsibilities that make it inappropriate to promote them to demanding positions. As one participant in a study of the federal workforce explained, "I mean, there were 2 or 3 names [of women] in the hat, and they said, 'I don't want to talk about her because she has children who are still home in these [evening] hours.' Now they don't pose that thing about men on the list, many of whom also have children in that age group."

Underinvestment in social capital

Perhaps the most destructive result of the work/family balancing act so many women must perform is that it leaves very little time for socializing with colleagues and building professional networks. The social capital that accrues from such "nonessential" parts of work turns out to be quite essential indeed. One study yielded the following description of managers who advanced rapidly in hierarchies: Fast-track managers "spent relatively more time and effort socializing, politicking, and interacting with outsiders than did their less successful counterparts. . .[and] did not give much time or attention to the traditional management activities of planning, decision making, and controlling or to the human resource management activities of motivating/reinforcing, staffing, training/developing, and managing conflict." This suggests that social capital is even more necessary to managers' advancement than skillful performance of traditional managerial tasks.

Even given sufficient time, women can find it difficult to engage in and benefit from informal networking if they are a small minority. In such settings, the influential networks are composed entirely or almost entirely of men. Breaking into those male networks can be hard, especially when men center their networks on masculine activities. The recent gender discrimination lawsuit against Wal-Mart provides examples of this. For instance, an executive retreat took the form of a quail-hunting expedition at Sam Walton's ranch in Texas. Middle managers' meetings included visits to strip clubs and Hooters restaurants, and a sales conference attended by thousands of store managers featured a football theme. One executive received feedback that she probably would not advance in the company because she didn't hunt or fish.

Management Interventions That Work

Taking the measure of the labyrinth that confronts women leaders, we see that it begins with prejudices that benefit men and penalize women, continues with particular resistance to women's leadership, includes questions of leadership style and authenticity, and—most dramatically for many women—features the challenge of balancing work and family responsibilities. It becomes clear that a woman's situation as she reaches her peak career years is the result of many turns at many challenging junctures. Only a few individual women have made the right combination of moves to land at the center of power—but as for the rest, there is usually no single turning point where their progress was diverted and the prize was lost.

What's to be done in the face of such a multifaceted problem? A solution that is often proposed is for governments to implement and enforce antidiscrimination legislation and thereby require organizations to eliminate inequitable practices. However, analysis of discrimination cases that have gone to court has shown that legal remedies can be elusive when gender inequality results from norms embedded in organizational structure and culture. The more effective approach is for organizations to appreciate the subtlety and complexity of the problem and to attack its many roots simultaneously. More specifically, if a company wants to see more women arrive in its executive suite, it should do the following:

Increase people's awareness of the psychological drivers of prejudice toward female leaders, and work to dispel those perceptions. Raising awareness of ingrained bias has been the aim of many diversity-training initiatives, and no doubt they have been more helpful than harmful. There is the danger they will be undermined, however, if their lessons are not underscored by what managers say and do in the course of day-to-day work.

Change the long-hours norm. Especially in the context of knowledge work, it can be hard to assess individuals' relative contributions, and managers may resort to "hours spent at work" as the prime indicator of someone's worth to the organization. To the extent an organization can shift the focus to objective measures of productivity, women with family demands on their time but highly productive work habits will receive the rewards and encouragement they deserve.

Reduce the subjectivity of performance evaluation. Greater objectivity in evaluations also combats the effects of lingering prejudice in both hiring and promotion. To ensure fairness, criteria should be explicit and evaluation processes designed to limit the influence of decision makers' conscious and unconscious biases.

Use open-recruitment tools, such as advertising and employment agencies, rather than relying on informal social networks and referrals

to fill positions. Recruitment from within organizations also should be transparent, with postings of open positions in appropriate venues. Research has shown that such personnel practices increase the numbers of women in managerial roles.

Ensure a critical mass of women in executive positions—not just one or two women—to head off the problems that come with tokenism. Token women tend to be pegged into narrow stereotypical roles such as "seductress," "mother," "pet," or "iron maiden." (Or more colorfully, as one woman banker put it, "When you start out in banking, you are a slut or a geisha.") Pigeonholing like this limits women's options and makes it difficult for them to rise to positions of responsibility. When women are not a small minority, their identities as women become less salient, and colleagues are more likely to react to them in terms of their individual competencies.

Avoid having a sole female member of any team. Top management tends to divide its small population of women managers among many projects in the interests of introducing diversity to them all. But several studies have found that, so outnumbered, the women tend to be ignored by the men. A female vice president of a manufacturing company described how, when she or another woman ventures an idea in a meeting, it tends to be overlooked: "It immediately gets lost in the conversation. Then two minutes later, a man makes the same suggestion, and it's 'Wow! What a great idea!' And you sit there and think, 'What just happened?'" As women reach positions of higher power and authority, they increasingly find themselves in gender-imbalanced groups—and some find themselves, for the first time, seriously marginalized. This is part of the reason that the glass ceiling metaphor resonates with so many. But in fact, the problem can be present at any level.

Help shore up social capital. As we've discussed, the call of family responsibilities is mainly to blame for women's underinvestment in networking. When time is scarce, this social activity is the first thing to go by the wayside. Organizations can help women appreciate why it deserves more attention. In particular, women gain from strong and supportive mentoring relationships and connections with powerful networks. When a well-placed individual who possesses greater legitimacy (often a man) takes an interest in a woman's career, her efforts to build social capital can proceed far more efficiently.

Prepare women for line management with appropriately demanding assignments. Women, like men, must have the benefit of developmental job experiences if they are to qualify for promotions. But, as one woman executive wrote, "Women have been shunted off into support areas for the last 30 years, rather than being in the business of doing business, so the pool of women trained to assume leadership positions in any large company is very small." Her point was that women should be taught in business school to insist on line jobs when they enter the workforce. One company that has taken up the challenge has been Procter & Gamble. According to a report by Claudia Deutsch in the *New York Times,* the company was experiencing an executive attrition rate that was twice as high for women as for men. Some of the women reported having to change companies to land jobs that provided challenging work. P&G's subsequent efforts to bring more women into line management both improved its overall retention of women and increased the number of women in senior management.

Establish family-friendly human resources practices. These may include flextime, job sharing, telecommuting, elder care provisions, adoption benefits, dependent child care options, and employee-sponsored on-site child care. Such support can allow women to stay in their jobs during the most demanding years of child rearing, build social capital, keep up to date in their fields, and eventually compete for higher positions. A study of 72 large U.S. firms showed (controlling for other variables) that family-friendly HR practices in place in 1994 increased the proportion of women in senior management over the subsequent five years.

Allow employees who have significant parental responsibility more time to prove themselves worthy of promotion. This recommendation is particularly directed to organizations, many of them professional services firms, that have established "up or out" career progressions. People not ready for promotion at the same time as the top performers in their cohort aren't simply left in place—they're asked to leave. But many parents (most often mothers), while fully capable of reaching that level of achievement, need extra time—perhaps a year or two—to get there. Forcing them off the promotion path not only reduces the number of women reaching top management positions, but also constitutes a failure by the firm to capitalize on its early investment in them.

Welcome women back. It makes sense to give high-performing women who step away from the workforce an opportunity to return to responsible positions when their circumstances change. Some companies have established "alumni" programs, often because they see former employees as potential sources of new business. A few companies have gone further to activate these networks for other purposes, as well. (Procter & Gamble taps alumni for innovation purposes; Booz Allen sees its alumni ranks as a source of subcontractors.) Keeping lines of communication open can convey the message that a return may be possible.

Encourage male participation in family-friendly benefits. Dangers lurk in family-friendly benefits that are used only by women. Exercising options such as generous parental leave and part-time work slows down women's careers. More profoundly, having many more women than men take such benefits can harm the careers of women in general because of the expectation that they may well exercise those options. Any effort toward greater family friendliness should actively recruit male participation to avoid inadvertently making it harder for women to gain access to essential managerial roles.

Managers can be forgiven if they find the foregoing list a tall order. It's a wide-ranging set of interventions and still far from exhaustive. The point, however, is just that: Organizations will succeed in filling half their top management slots with women—and women who are the true performance equals of their male counterparts—only by attacking all the reasons they are absent today. Glass ceiling–inspired programs and projects can do just so much if the leakage of talented women is happening on every lower floor of the building. Individually, each of these interventions has been shown to make a difference. Collectively, we believe, they can make all the difference.

The View from Above

Imagine visiting a formal garden and finding within it a high hedgerow. At a point along its vertical face, you spot a rectangle—a neatly pruned and inviting doorway. Are you aware as you step through that you are entering a labyrinth? And, three doorways later, as the reality of the puzzle settles in, do you have any idea how to proceed? This is the situation in which many women find themselves in their career endeavors. Ground-level perplexity and frustration make every move uncertain.

Labyrinths become infinitely more tractable when seen from above. When the eye can take in the whole of the puzzle—the starting position, the goal, and the maze of walls—solutions begin to suggest themselves. This has been the goal of our research. Our hope is that women, equipped with a map of the barriers they will confront on their path to professional achievement, will make more informed choices. We hope that managers, too, will understand where their efforts can facilitate the progress of women. If women are to achieve equality, women and men will have to share leadership equally. With a greater understanding of what stands in the way of gender-balanced leadership, we draw nearer to attaining it in our time.

Originally published in September 2007. Reprint R0709C

Adapted from *Through the Labyrinth: The Truth About How Women Become Leaders* by Alice H. Eagly and Linda L. Carli (Boston: Harvard Business School Press, 2007).

Do Women Lack Ambition?

by Anna Fels

"I WONDERED, BEFORE I CAME HERE, whether I was going to confess to you this secret I've had since I was seven. I haven't even told my husband about it." The woman across from me, a journalist in her forties, paused and looked at me intently, trying to decide whether she should go on. Sitting there under her worried gaze, I wondered where we were going with this. As a psychiatrist, I'm used to hearing the most improbable and even lurid of personal revelations. But this woman was not a patient. She was a friend of a friend, who had kindly agreed to let me interview her. It was actually the first in a series of exploratory discussions I had scheduled as a start to my research on ambition in women's lives, and I had already found myself in unfamiliar territory. How had my seemingly straightforward question about childhood goals elicited a long-hidden secret?

The journalist looked at me uncertainly but continued. "When I was about seven, I had a notebook at school, and I would write poems and stories in it and illustrate them. . . . I had this acronym that was like magic, like a secret pact with myself. I didn't even tell my sisters its meaning. It was IWBF—I Will Be Famous." She broke into nervous laughter. "Oh my God, I can't believe I told you. You must understand: I didn't want to be recognized in the streets. My pact was tied up with writing and being recognized for it. I'm sure it was tied up with my father's approval and the literary world he operated in."

This was the long-held secret? Not sex, lies, or videotape, but an odd incantation from childhood? It was the first of what were to be many lessons for me on how hidden and emotion laden the subject of ambition is for women. I soon came to realize that although the articulate, educated group of women I interviewed could cogently and calmly talk about topics ranging from money to sex, when the subject of ambition arose, the level of intensity took a quantum leap.

In fact, the women I interviewed hated the very word. For them, "ambition" necessarily implied egotism, selfishness, self-aggrandizement, or the manipulative use of others for one's own ends. None of them would admit to being ambitious. Instead, the constant refrain was "It's not me; it's the work." "It's not about me; it's about helping children." "I hate to promote myself. I'd rather be in my work-shop alone." You could write off such comments as social convention or mere window dressing if it weren't for two facts. First, men simply do not talk this way. (Quite the contrary: The men I interviewed considered ambition a necessary and desirable part of their lives.) Second, the statements weren't tossed off casually. Clearly, these accomplished women were caught up in some sort of fear. But of what?

The Two Faces of Ambition

As I tried to sort through the diverse responses to my questions and to home in on the aspect of ambition that made these women so uncomfortable, I realized I needed to backtrack. First I had to understand what ambition consisted of—for men and for women.

In psychiatry, as in most branches of science, the study of a complex phenomenon often begins with researchers tracing it to its earliest, simplest form. So I decided to review the childhood ambitions recalled by the women I had interviewed. Compared with the wordy, ambivalent responses these women had given about their current ambitions, their childhood ambitions were direct and clear. They had a delightfully unapologetic sense of grandiosity and limitless possibility. Each of the women had pictured herself in an important role: a great American novelist, an Olympic figure skater, a famous actress, president of the United States, a fashion designer, a rock star, a diplomat.

In nearly all of the childhood ambitions, two undisguised elements were joined together. One was mastery of a special skill: writing, dancing, acting, diplomacy. The other was recognition: attention from an appreciative audience. Looking through studies on the development of both boys and girls, I noticed that they virtually always identified the same two components of childhood ambition. There was a plan that involved a real accomplishment requiring work and skill, and there was an expectation of approval in the form of fame, status, acclaim, praise, or honor.

That the first of these—mastery—was fundamental to ambition seemed nearly incontrovertible. Without mastery, a picture of the future isn't an ambition; it's simply wishful thinking. (You may desperately want to win the lottery, but that's not an ambition.) Approximately half a century after Freud postulated his "drive theory" of motivation based on sex and aggression, researchers and theoreticians alike realized that a huge portion of behavior simply could not be explained in those terms. Jean Piaget and other developmental psychologists who focused on children's need to master both intellectual and motor tasks discovered that children would repeat a task over and over until they could predict and determine the outcome. Theorists such as Erik Erikson began to posit that at a certain stage, children develop a "sense of industry," or the need to do things well, even perfectly. Robert White, one of the seminal investigators of motivation, named this drive toward mastery "effectance." "It is characteristic of this particular sort of activity," White noted, "that it is selective, directed, and persistent, and that an instrumental act will be learned for the sole reward of engaging in it."

In Frank Conroy's classic memoir of his childhood, *Stop-Time*, the author captures the sheer joy that children, like adults, take in mastery. The young Conroy becomes fascinated with the yo-yo and painstakingly works through a book of tricks, practicing hour after hour in the woods near his house:

> "The greatest pleasure in yo-yoing was an abstract pleasure—watching the dramatization of simple physical laws, and realizing they would never fail if a trick was done correctly. . . .

I remember the first time I did a particularly lovely trick. . . . My pleasure at that moment was as much from the beauty of the experiment as from pride."

Doing a thing well can be a reward in and of itself. The delight provided by the skill repays the effort of learning it. But the pursuit of mastery over an extended period of time requires a specific context: An evaluating, encouraging audience must be present for skills to develop. Conroy, in the same childhood scene, rushes off to show his new yo-yoing expertise to his friends and to two particularly proficient older boys. It is vital for the expertise to be recognized by others.

We are not used to thinking of recognition as a fundamental emotional need, particularly in adulthood. It's nice when you get it, but if you don't, it's not the end of the world—life goes on. We even tend to look down on those whose eagerness for recognition is too obvious, too pressing. And in truth, some people have needs for recognition that are exaggerated and nearly insatiable; they require constant infusions of admiration to maintain their tenuous sense of self-worth. In psychiatry, such individuals are called narcissists.

But multiple areas of research have demonstrated that recognition is one of the motivational engines that drives the development of almost any type of skill. Far from being a pleasant but largely inessential response, it is one of the most basic of human requirements. We all want our efforts and accomplishments to be acknowledged.

In the typical learning cycle, recognition fuels the next stage of learning. The early-learning theorist Albert Bandura was clear on this point: "Young children imitate accurately when they have incentives to do so, but their imitations deteriorate rapidly if others do not care how they behave."

And what's true in childhood is no less true in later life. Research has confirmed that in the overwhelming majority of cases, the acquisition of expertise requires recognition. A rare longitudinal study by the renowned psychologist Jerome Kagan looked specifically at this issue. He and his coauthor, Howard Moss, examined the relationship between "the tendency to strive for a mastery of selected skills (achievement behavior) and social recognition through acquisition of specific goals or behaviors." They followed a cohort from childhood through adulthood, and at the end of this massive project concluded that there was a high positive correlation between mastery and recognition. According to Kagan and Moss, "it may be impossible to measure the 'desire to improve a skill' independent of the individual's 'desire for recognition.'"

Without earned affirmation, long-term learning and performance are rarely achieved. Ambitions are both the product of and, later on, the source of affirmation.

What's Dashing Women's Dreams?

There is no evidence that the desires to acquire skills and to receive affirmation for accomplishments are less present in women than in men. So why is it that we find such dramatic differences between men and women in their attitudes toward ambition and in how they create, reconfigure, and realize (or abandon) their goals?

One clue to the pressures that contemporary women experience in connection with their ambitions can be found in the stories that unusually successful women tell about their lives. In their best-selling book *See Jane Win: The Rimm Report on How 1,000 Girls Became Successful Women,* Sylvia Rimm and her coauthors, after profiling a state senator, remark with puzzlement, "[The senator], like many of the women of our study, attributes much of her success to luck." In another chapter, the authors quote an eminent female chairman of a department of medicine as concluding, "Everything has been rather serendipitous. None of what I've described to you was planned. . . . I was able to get good positions and good things just happened." An interview from a women's magazine with one of the most famous women architects in America revealed the intensity of the woman's dread about receiving attention. The magazine reported: "Laurinda Spear is so riddled with anxiety about the way she might come across in print that she endlessly repeats the same self-deprecating refrain: 'Can't you just say that I'm this totally bumbling person?'"

Hidden in Plain View

IT'S NO SECRET THAT WOMEN receive less recognition for their accomplishments than men do. The documentation is substantial, and the findings are consistent.

Preschool

By nursery school, the differential in attention received by girls and boys is already evident. In one representative study of 15 coed preschool classrooms, investigators found that "all 15 of the teachers gave more attention to boys. . . . They got both more physical and verbal rewards. Boys also received more direction from the teachers and were twice as likely as the girls to get individual instruction on how to do things."

Grammar School

Studies show that in grammar school, girls have stronger verbal skills than boys do. One might assume that this would serve girls well, but they continue to get less recognition than boys. One three-year project looked at more than 100 fourth-, sixth-, and eighth-grade classrooms in four states and the District of Columbia. The conclusion: "Teachers praise boys more than girls, give boys more academic help, and are more likely to accept boys' comments during classroom discussions." In high school, the pattern becomes even more pronounced, particularly in math and the sciences.

College

In the late 1980s, a women's college that was in the process of becoming coed videotaped and analyzed coed classes elsewhere to "make sure that the quality of the women's education would not be affected." To quote the abstract of the resulting paper:

> "Do men get more for their money than women when they invest four years and tens of thousands of dollars in a college education? Close examination of videotapes of classroom interactions reveals that they generally do. . . . Should a teacher choose a first volunteer to answer a question (as often happens), that student will most likely be male. . . .

One could chalk up these demurrals (and I heard many of them in my own interviews) to women's innate modesty or even see them as a sly way of highlighting their achievements. But the fear, at times verging on panic, that women express when they are personally recognized for their work belies this interpretation.

Tacit collaboration of faculty members permits men to dominate class discussions disproportionately to their numbers."

Graduate School

One study found that in graduate school, women "are more likely to be teaching assistants rather than research assistants, as compared to men, and receive, on the average, less financial support."

First Jobs

Several studies have looked at the effect of gender on recognition in the workplace. Here is a summary from one such investigation:

> "Two groups of people were asked to evaluate particular items, such as articles, paintings, résumés, and the like. The names attached to the items given each group of evaluators were clearly either male or female, but reversed for each group—that is, what one group believed was originated by a man, the other believed was originated by a woman. Regardless of the items, when they were ascribed to a man, they were rated higher than when they were ascribed to a woman. In all of these studies, women evaluators were as likely as men to downgrade those items ascribed to women."

Career

In one study, male and female researchers took turns assuming leader and nonleader roles with subjects performing a problem-solving task. The researchers found that regardless of which role the woman took,

> "The trained females received a greater number of negative facial reactions than positive ones. . . . When women [were] assertive and acted as leaders the negative reactions outnumbered the positive ones; women end up with a net loss. . . . The naive participants [the subjects] paid less attention to the women than the men; for example, they made fewer facial reactions to the women per minute of talking time."

It seems paradoxical. Women have gained hard-won access to training in nearly all fields, and this type of expertise can bring enormous satisfaction. But far from celebrating their achievements in newly available professions, women too frequently seek to deflect attention from themselves. They refuse to claim a central, purposeful place in their own stories, eagerly shifting the credit elsewhere and shunning recognition. Furthermore, on close inspection, it emerges that it's not only women of achievement who anxiously work to relinquish recognition—it's nearly all women. Studies have demonstrated that the daily texture of women's lives from childhood on is infiltrated with microencounters in which quiet withdrawal and the ceding of available attention to others is expected—particularly in the presence of men.

It's tempting to conclude, as many have, that women aren't actually deferring to others when they remove themselves from the spotlight; they're just intrinsically different in their needs and style. Women, after all, may just be less interested in personal attention than men. Or maybe they simply don't care about the types of recognition that men strive for. It has been suggested, for example, that women have a greater capacity for empathy than men, making it more painful for them not to gratify the wishes of others or relinquish coveted resources. (And recognition is nothing if not a coveted social resource.)

The belief that women's deferential behavior with regard to recognition is "natural" has not held up in the extensive research on gender that has been conducted since the 1970s. By and large, the research has suggested that to a significant degree, such behavior varies according to social context: Girls and women more openly seek and compete for affirmation when they are with other women—for example, in sports or in all-girl academic settings. They have no difficulty aggressively pursuing roles that complement rather than compete with males (such as trying out for a female acting part, a modeling career, or a singing group). But they change their behaviors when it comes to competing directly with men.

Intuitively, we know this is true. As the recent best seller *The Rules: Time-Tested Secrets for Capturing the Heart of Mr. Right* tells women, "Don't be a loud, knee-slapping, hysterically funny girl. This is O.K. when you're alone with your girlfriend. But when you're with a man you like, be quiet and mysterious. . . . Don't talk so much. . . . Look into his eyes, be attentive and a good listener so he knows you are a caring being—a person who would make a supportive wife." The book later acknowledges, "Of course, this is not how you really feel. This is how you pretend to feel until it feels real." (For more scientific evidence of women's invisibility in situations that involve men, see the sidebar "Hidden in Plain View.")

Hidden Barriers

Although women are no longer denied access to training in most types of careers, they have come up against what seems to be an even more powerful barrier to their ambitions. In both the public and the private spheres, white, middle-class women are facing the reality that in order to be seen as feminine, they must provide or relinquish resources—including recognition—to others. It is difficult for women to confront and address the unspoken mandate that they subordinate needs for recognition to those of others—particularly men. The expectation is so deeply rooted in the culture's ideals of femininity that it is largely unconscious.

In the psychological instruments used for studies of gender, however, such expectations are made explicit. The most famous and widely applied psychological measure of femininity (as well as of masculinity and androgyny) is the revised Bem Sex Role Inventory (BSRI). The test includes 60 descriptive adjectives—20 masculine traits, 20 feminine traits, and 20 neutral traits—that subjects use to rate themselves. These traits were originally chosen from 200 personality characteristics by 100 male and female undergraduates at Stanford University in the 1970s. The students, mostly white and middle-class, were asked to rank the desirability of these traits for men and women in American society. The traits chosen to define femininity in the BSRI are: yielding, loyal, cheerful, compassionate, shy, sympathetic, affectionate, sensitive to the needs of others, flatterable, understanding, eager to soothe hurt feelings, soft-spoken, warm, tender, gullible, childlike, does not use harsh language, loves children, gentle, and (somewhat redundantly) femininity.

Reading through these adjectives, two basic tenets of femininity emerge. The first is that femininity exists only in the context of a relationship. A woman's sexual identity is based on qualities that can't be expressed in isolation. To quote the author Jane Smiley, "Does a woman alone in a dark room feel like a woman? . . . How about a woman reading a book or climbing mountains?"

The second tenet that emerges from the BSRI adjectives is that a woman must be providing something for the other person, be that person a lover, a child, a sick parent, a husband, or even a boss. Giving is the chief activity that defines femininity. This may help explain why professional women are credited with being highly supportive managers and excellent team players. By focusing their energy on these aspects of work life, women can be both business-like and feminine.

Near the top of the list of resources that women are asked to provide is recognition. They are asked both to supply personal recognition for their husbands and to relinquish recognition in the work sphere to the men with whom they work. When women speak as much as men in a work situation or compete for high-visibility positions, their femininity is routinely assailed. They are caricatured as either asexual and unattractive or promiscuous and seductive. Something must be wrong with their sexuality.

Masculinity, by contrast, is defined neither by relationships nor by what men provide for others—except financially. One can be masculine in solitary splendor. The BSRI adjectives that describe masculinity are: self-reliant, strong personality, forceful, independent, analytical, defends one's beliefs, athletic, assertive, has leadership abilities, willing to take risks, makes decisions easily, self-sufficient, dominant, willing to take a stand, aggressive, acts as a leader, individualistic, competitive, ambitious. ("Masculinity" is the twentieth trait.) The "other" appears in these adjectives chiefly as someone against or over whom the man must assert himself. Not only can a man be solitary and masculine, but if he's in a relationship that involves overt dependence or being influenced by others (and virtually all relationships do), his sexual identity is at risk.

College women have been shown to identify with more of these masculine traits in recent years than they have in the past—without dropping any of the feminine ones. These young women have, for example, been found to endorse goals such as becoming an authority in one's field, obtaining recognition from colleagues, having administrative responsibilities, and being better off financially. But it is unclear how this apparently broadened gender role plays out in their actual lives. As the author of one study notes, "Soliciting the respondent's expected career goals at only one point in time at such an early period in the individual's life tells us very little about the degree of commitment attached to these career goals."

At each historical juncture where women have achieved access to social influence and recognition—legal and political rights, educational opportunities, career options—their capacity to be "real women" has been impugned. They are labeled as bluestockings or spinsters or agamic (the Victorian term for women who pursued higher education and were therefore considered asexual). In the present, this painful questioning occurs when career women move beyond the student or early career stage and are trying to start families. Many articles and books caution that career women will fail to get married, or, if they do get married, will be unable to have children—or if they do have children, will be bad mothers. They will somehow fail to fulfill the feminine role. The data on which these "facts" are largely based do not support the conclusions. But for women, they raise an understandably frightening specter.

Clearly, there are many situations in which both the masculine and feminine BSRI traits are compatible and even complementary. You can, for example, be a dynamic leader who is also sensitive and responsive to the needs of your staff. But there are also scenarios in which the traits inevitably conflict. Such conflicts arise when jobs become more competitive and when couples begin to have children. Increasingly precious and limited resources must be allocated: time for work, for leisure, for financial independence, for career advancement, and for power. It is precisely at this time in a woman's early adulthood that the mandates of traditional femininity reemerge in full force. Women must decide whether to subordinate their needs to those of their male partners and colleagues. What should a young married woman do if her husband wants to move overseas to advance his career even if it disrupts or derails her own? Should she be "yielding," "loyal" and "cheerful," or should

Getting Ambitious About Ambition

WHAT CAN BE DONE IN THE FACE of the overwhelming odds stacked against women's ambitions? Here are some recommendations and observations.

Organize

Women must see themselves as a political constituency (one that encompasses the majority of voters) with one set of goals in particular: the support of mothers in the workforce as well as mothers who choose to remain at home with their children. Women will be able to fully share in the satisfaction that ambitions can provide only when they are confident that their children are well cared for.

Don't Expect Things to Fall into Place

Because so little is mapped out for them at this moment in time, women, more than men, need to actively imagine themselves into their futures. Unlike men, women have few accepted roles in our society—or, more accurately, they have too many: innovative professional, devoted mother, competent employee, sexually attractive babe, supportive wife, talented homemaker, and independent wage earner, to name a few. It falls nearly entirely on the individual woman to carve out a life for herself with adequate meaning and satisfaction—not an easy task for anyone, let alone an impressionable young person. For each woman, life must be a creation of sorts and also an assertion of values, priorities, and identity, because no role is unquestioningly accepted in our society.

Provide for Structures of Recognition

To sustain their ambitions, women must formulate life plans that include the potential for receiving earned recognition—and that recognition must

she be "independent" and "forceful"? What happens when her partner's meetings last later and later, and there's no parent home with the children unless she leaves the workplace early? Should she be understanding and sensitive to the needs of others (feminine) or willing to take a stand (masculine)? What happens when a previously supportive male mentor finds a more proactive, independent, or competitive stance alienating?

Women have greater opportunities for forming and pursuing their own goals now than at any time in history. But doing so is socially condoned only if they have first satisfied the needs of all their family members: husbands, children, elderly parents, and others. If this primarily be based on talent, skill, or work, rather than on appearance, sexual availability, or subservience. This means identifying, critically assessing, and purposefully developing "spheres of recognition" that can provide sustaining affirmation. If we have no opportunities for appropriate support, we have to acknowledge this and find other venues. Otherwise, the situation is not only a dead end but one that will engender painful and unnecessary self-doubt.

Blow Your Own Horn

Even when discriminatory factors are not at play, women have much more difficulty than men developing relationships with people who have the power to advance their work. Actively pursuing advantageous connections runs counter to the classic ideal of femininity. Women in virtually every profession express their distaste for cultivating such relationships, labeling it as "pushy." Unfortunately, there is ample data that in and of itself, high-caliber work is unlikely to produce proper recognition for accomplishments.

Realize It's Never Too Late

As profoundly social beings, we work throughout life to maximize affirmation. In some ways, this is a disturbing realization; we would like to believe that by the time we reach adulthood our goals are formed and we are largely self-motivated. The available research, however, does not support this view. To an astonishing extent, opportunity for mastery and recognition continually re-shapes our ambitions and modulates the effort we expend on them. Powerful mentors, opportunities for learning new skills, promotions, admiring peers who provide collegial support, institutional recognition, and broad cultural trends all continuously mold ambitions. At what point does ambition become fixed? In short: never.

requirement isn't met, women's ambitions as well as their femininity will be called into question.

In addition, for a woman's ambition to thrive, both the development of expertise and the recognition of accomplishments outside of the family are required. The elimination of the barriers that have historically kept women from mastering a subject—such as restrictions on admission to professional schools or the habit of doing business and advancing careers inside men-only clubs—has brought women a long way toward realizing their ambitions. But the pressure on girls and women to relinquish opportunities for recognition in the workplace continues to have powerful repercussions.

One key type of discrimination that women face is the expectation that "feminine" women will forfeit opportunities for recognition at home and at work. Being silenced or ignored often remains a baffling and frustrating barrier to women's understanding of how their lives are shaped. This is a "sin of omission" rather than one of commission, so it's hard to spot. It's not as obvious as being denied the right to vote or access to birth control. Women tend to feel foolish asking for appropriate acknowledgement of their contributions. They find it difficult to demand appropriate support—in the form of time, money, or promotion—to pursue their own goals. They feel selfish when they do not subordinate their needs to those of others.

This subtle, incremental, but ultimately powerful dynamic militates against women's pursuit and attainment of their goals in most fields. For them, or for anyone, the motivation to learn a skill or to pursue any endeavor, including an ambition, can be roughly calculated on the basis of two factors: how certain the person is that he or she will be able to attain the desired goal and how valued the expected rewards are.

The rewards aspect of this calculation is problematic for women. Although they may find mastery as satisfying as do their male peers, the social rewards that women can expect to reap for their skills are diminished. The personal and societal recognition they receive for their accomplishments is quantitatively poorer, qualitatively more ambivalent, and, perhaps most discouraging, less predictable.

It gets worse. To attempt to master a skill, particularly one that requires prolonged effort, you must believe you are likely to succeed. And here we see the long-term impact of the relatively low recognition that girls and young women receive. Despite the fact that girls' and women's achievements, particularly in the academic sphere, frequently outstrip those of their male peers, they routinely underestimate their abilities. Boys and men, by contrast, have repeatedly been shown to have an inflated estimation of their capabilities. Paradoxically, these inaccurate self-ratings by both women and men seem to be accurate reflections of the praise and recognition they receive for their efforts. The impact of these findings on the selection and pursuit of an ambition is obvious: If you don't think the chances are great that you will reach a career goal, you won't attempt to reach it—even if the rewards are highly desirable.

This, for women, is why early aspirations so often do not translate into achievement later in life: A lack of appropriate affirmation of accomplishments in combination with threats to women's sexual identity inevitably lead to demoralization. And so the process continues. At many junctures in their lives, both women and men must reevaluate the meaning and value of their ambitions and decide how intensely to pursue them. But when women revisit their calculations, they are more likely than men to conclude that their goals aren't rewarding enough to justify the effort required to reach them. So they abandon their ambitions. Sociologists who have compared middle-class females' goals to their actual situations in midlife have found the correlation to be surprisingly weak. As one author discovered, "Women are only slightly more likely to follow the paths they expect to [early on] than not."

Set Up for a Fall

Where does this leave contemporary women? Over many decades, opportunities for women have slowly increased through the different life stages, starting with girlhood and working up to young womanhood. Access to grammar school education for girls was followed by access to high school and college programs. By the early twentieth century, a few women had gained admission to graduate and professional schools, and in the 1970s, women began to graduate from these programs in significant numbers. By the 1980s and 1990s, women were assuming places in the lower ranks of the professions in ever-greater numbers.

Today, the time when women become second-class citizens, when their options are radically reduced in comparison with those of men, has been pushed yet later into their lives. Girls and women still receive less favorable treatment than their male counterparts throughout their childhoods and adolescence—but the discrepancy has narrowed. Many young, middle-class women have experienced a shift toward more equal opportunities right up to their early careers and marriages.

Women now experience the most powerful social and institutional discrimination during their twenties and early thirties, after they have left the educational system and started pursuing their ambitions. At the age when women most frequently marry and have children, they must decide whether to try to hold on to their own ambitions or downsize or abandon them. Often, a young woman must make this decision at the moment when she is just learning to be a parent, with all its attendant fears, pleasures, insecurities—and around-the-clock work.

As with past obstacles women have faced, the current ones have proved stressful, confusing, and painful. In all such transitions, there are no easy solutions. Institutional changes and cultural norms lag behind social realities. The lack of adequate social support, ongoing career opportunities, and financial protection for women who provide child care is the contemporary phase of women's long struggle for equal rights.

Stressed for Success

As contemporary women evaluate their goals, they must decide how much of the stress that comes with ambition they are willing to tolerate. I have vivid memories of being among the first large wave of women medical students and doctors. My first interviewer for medical school, a surgeon, asked antagonistically how I could possibly care for my children. In medical school, many of the physicians who taught us were openly hostile to women students. I recall a lecture on endometriosis entitled "The Working Woman's Disease." The hospital didn't even have uniforms that fit us: For a while, we all looked like little girls dressed up in Daddy's clothes. When my female peers and I moved on to our residencies and fellowships in our early thirties, there were no established policies about pregnancy leave, no options for part-time work, no available child care. I gave birth to one of my children after finishing my patient rounds at nine o'clock at night. Luckily, the delivery room was across the street. At that historical moment, becoming a physician was a brutal, confusing, and often demoralizing process for a woman.

Twenty years later, many of the problems my colleagues and I faced have been addressed. But in this field, as in many others, the most intense social pressures are no longer about mastery. Hardly anyone claims today that women lack the native ability to become neurosurgeons or executives. And the problems don't tend to arise in college or in the first few years of a career. These days, the threat to women's ambitions comes at a later phase of women's lives, when they have families and are advancing to more competitive positions in their work. Women who pursue careers must cope with jobs structured to accommodate the life cycles of men with wives who don't have full-time careers. And they must suffer the social pressure to fulfill more traditional, "feminine" roles. It's a situation that still creates unnecessarily agonizing choices. Too often, when the choice must be made, women choose to downsize their ambitions or abandon them altogether. As at each prior time when women gained new opportunities, the early stages of change are exhilarating, but also painful.

Interestingly, many famous writers have claimed that in later life, after their children have been raised, women develop a new resilience and energy. Dorothy Sayers referred to such women as "uncontrollable by any earthly force." Margaret Mead described an age of "heightened vitality" that she called the Third Age. Isak Dinesen proclaimed, "Women . . . when they are old enough to have done with the business of being a woman, and can let loose their strength, must be the most powerful creatures in the whole world." I have often wondered whether the newfound strength of these women reflects the fact that their sexual identity is no longer assailable. "Been there, done that," they can say to anyone who questions their capacity for relationships. The classic reproach (always aimed at women and never at men)—that they are promoting themselves at the expense of others who need their care—no longer applies. In a very real sense, it is the first time in their lives that they are free to express, without fear of reprisal, the wide spectrum of feelings and behaviors previously reserved for men.

Originally published in April 2004. Reprint R0404B

Adapted from *Necessary Dreams: Ambition in Women's Changing Lives* by Anna Fels (New York: Pantheon, 2004).

Women Rising

The Unseen Barriers. *by Herminia Ibarra, Robin Ely, and Deborah Kolb*

MANY CEOS WHO MAKE GENDER diversity a priority—by setting aspirational goals for the proportion of women in leadership roles, insisting on diverse slates of candidates for senior positions, and developing mentoring and training programs—are frustrated. They and their companies spend time, money, and good intentions on efforts to build a more robust pipeline of upwardly mobile women, and then not much happens.

The problem with these leaders' approaches is that they don't address the often fragile process of coming to see oneself, and to be seen by others, as a leader. Becoming a leader involves much more than being put in a leadership role, acquiring new skills, and adapting one's style to the requirements of that role. It involves a fundamental identity shift. Organizations inadvertently undermine this process when they advise women to proactively seek leadership roles without also addressing policies and practices that communicate a mismatch between how women are seen and the qualities and experiences people tend to associate with leaders.

A significant body of research (see "Further Reading") shows that for women, the subtle gender bias that persists in organizations and in society disrupts the learning cycle at the heart of becoming a leader. This research also points to some steps that companies can take in order to rectify the situation. It's not enough to identify and instill the "right" skills and competencies as if in a social vacuum.

The context must support a woman's motivation to lead and also increase the likelihood that others will recognize and encourage her efforts—even when she doesn't look or behave like the current generation of senior executives.

The solutions to the pipeline problem are very different from what companies currently employ. Traditional high-potential, mentoring, and leadership education programs are necessary but not sufficient. Our research, teaching, and consulting reveal three additional actions companies can take to improve the chances that women will gain a sense of themselves as leaders, be recognized as such, and ultimately succeed. (This article expands on our paper "Taking Gender into Account: Theory and Design for Women's Leadership Development Programs," *Academy of Management Learning & Education,* September 2011.)

Becoming a Leader

People become leaders by *internalizing a leadership identity* and *developing a sense of purpose.* Internalizing a sense of oneself as a leader is an iterative process. A person asserts leadership by taking purposeful action—such as convening a meeting to revive a dormant project. Others affirm or resist the action, thus encouraging or discouraging subsequent assertions. These interactions inform the person's sense of self as a leader and communicate how others view his or her fitness for the role.

As a person's leadership capabilities grow and opportunities to demonstrate them expand, high-profile, challenging assignments and other organizational endorsements become more likely. Such affirmation gives the person the fortitude to step outside a comfort zone and experiment with unfamiliar behaviors and new ways of exercising leadership. An absence of affirmation, however, diminishes self-confidence and discourages him or her from seeking developmental opportunities or experimenting. Leadership identity, which begins as a tentative, peripheral aspect of the self, eventually withers away, along with opportunities to grow through new assignments and real achievements. Over time, an aspiring leader acquires a reputation as having—or not having—high potential.

Idea in Brief

The Baseline

People become leaders iteratively: They shoulder increasingly challenging roles, learn from mentors, and experiment with new behaviors. Then, if their performance is affirmed, they repeat the process.

What the Research Shows

That process is often more difficult for women than for men because of subtle biases. For example,

behavior considered assertive in a man is seen as aggressive in a woman and thus denigrated rather than rewarded.

The Path Forward

Just naming those biases can help men and women alike to understand what's going on. That frees women to focus more on leadership purpose and less on how they're perceived.

The story of an investment banker we'll call Amanda is illustrative. Amanda's career stalled when she was in her thirties. Her problem, she was told, was that she lacked "presence" with clients (who were mostly older men) and was not sufficiently outspoken in meetings. Her career prospects looked bleak. But both her reputation and her confidence grew when she was assigned to work with two clients whose CFOs happened to be women. These women appreciated Amanda's smarts and the skillful way she handled their needs and concerns. Each in her own way started taking the initiative to raise Amanda's profile. One demanded that she be present at all key meetings, and the other refused to speak to anyone but Amanda when she called—actions that enhanced Amanda's credibility within her firm. "In our industry," Amanda explains, "having the key client relationship is everything." Her peers and supervisors began to see her not just as a competent project manager but as a trusted client adviser—an important prerequisite for promotion. These relationships, both internal and external, gave Amanda the confidence boost she needed to generate ideas and express them forthrightly, whether to colleagues or to clients. Her supervisors happily concluded that Amanda had finally shed her "meek and mild-mannered" former self and "stepped up" to leadership.

Effective leaders develop a sense of purpose by pursuing goals that align with their personal values and advance the collective good. This allows them to look beyond the status quo to what is *possible* and gives them a compelling reason to take action despite personal fears and insecurities. Such leaders are seen as authentic and trustworthy because they are willing to take risks in the service of shared goals. By connecting others to a larger purpose, they inspire commitment, boost resolve, and help colleagues find deeper meaning in their work.

Integrating leadership into one's core identity is particularly challenging for women, who must establish credibility in a culture that is deeply conflicted about whether, when, and how they should exercise authority. Practices that equate leadership with behaviors considered more common in men suggest that women are simply not cut out to be leaders. Furthermore, the human tendency to gravitate to people like oneself leads powerful men to sponsor and advocate for other men when leadership opportunities arise. As Amanda's story illustrates, women's leadership potential sometimes shows in less conventional ways—being responsive to clients' needs, for example, rather than boldly asserting a point of view—and sometimes it takes powerful women to recognize that potential. But powerful women are scarce.

Despite a lack of discriminatory intent, subtle, "second-generation" forms of workplace gender bias can obstruct the leadership identity development of a company's entire population of women. (See the sidebar "What Is Second-Generation Gender Bias?") The resulting underrepresentation of women in top positions reinforces entrenched beliefs, prompts and supports men's bids for leadership, and thus maintains the status quo.

The three actions we suggest to support women's access to leadership positions are (1) educate women and men about second-generation gender bias, (2) create safe "identity workspaces" to support transitions to bigger roles, and (3) anchor women's development efforts in a sense of leadership purpose rather than in how women are perceived. These actions will give women insight into themselves and their organizations, enabling them to more effectively chart a course to leadership.

Educate Everyone About Second-Generation Gender Bias

For women

More than 25 years ago the social psychologist Faye Crosby stumbled on a surprising phenomenon: Most women are unaware of having personally been victims of gender discrimination and deny it *even when it is objectively true and they see that women in general experience it.*

Many women have worked hard to take gender out of the equation—to simply be recognized for their skills and talents. Moreover, the existence of gender bias in organizational policies and practices may suggest that they have no power to determine their own success. When asked what might be holding women back in their organizations, they say:

"It's nothing overt. I just feel less of a connection, either positive or negative, with the guys I work with. So sometimes I seem to have difficulty getting traction for my ideas."

"I look around and see that my male colleagues have P&L responsibility and most of us are in staff roles. I was advised to make the move to a staff role after the birth of my second child. It would be easier, I was told. But now I recognize that there is no path back to the line."

"My firm has the very best intentions when it comes to women. But it seems every time a leadership role opens up, women are not on the slate. The claim is made that they just can't find women with the right skill set and experience."

These statements belie the notion that gender bias is absent from these women's work lives. Second-generation bias does not require an intent to exclude; nor does it necessarily produce direct, immediate harm to any individual. Rather, it creates a context—akin to "something in the water"—in which women fail to thrive or reach their full potential. Feeling less connected to one's male colleagues, being advised to take a staff role to accommodate family, finding oneself excluded from consideration for key positions—all these situations reflect work structures and practices that put women at a disadvantage.

WHAT IS SECOND-GENERATION GENDER BIAS?

RESEARCH HAS MOVED AWAY from a focus on the deliberate exclusion of women and toward investigating "second-generation" forms of gender bias as the primary cause of women's persistent underrepresentation in leadership roles. This bias erects powerful but subtle and often invisible barriers for women that arise from cultural assumptions and organizational structures, practices, and patterns of interaction that inadvertently benefit men while putting women at a disadvantage. Among them are:

A Paucity of Role Models for Women
Aspiring leaders need role models whose styles and behaviors they can experiment with and evaluate according to their own standards and others' reactions. Fewer female leaders means fewer role models and can suggest to young would-be leaders that being a woman is a liability—thus discouraging them from viewing senior women as credible sources of advice and support.

Gendered Career Paths and Gendered Work
Many entrenched organizational structures and work practices were designed to fit men's lives and situations at a time when women made up only a very small portion of the workforce. For one example, formal rotations in sales or operations have traditionally been a key step on the path to senior leadership, and men are more likely than women to have held such jobs. Yet requirements like these may be outdated when it comes to the kinds of experience that best prepare a person to lead. For another, career-enhancing international posts often assume a "trailing spouse" who has no career and can easily move—a family situation much more common for men than for women. How work is valued may similarly give men an advantage: Research indicates that organizations tend to ignore or undervalue behind-the-scenes work (building a team, avoiding a crisis), which women are more likely to do, while rewarding heroic work, which is most often done by men. These practices were not designed to

Without an understanding of second-generation bias, people are left with stereotypes to explain why women as a group have failed to achieve parity with men: If they can't reach the top, it is because they "don't ask," are "too nice," or simply "opt out." These messages tell women who have managed to succeed that they are exceptions and women who have experienced setbacks that it is their own fault for failing to be sufficiently aggressive or committed to the job.

be discriminatory, but their cumulative effect disadvantages women. A vicious cycle ensues: Men appear to be best suited to leadership roles, and this perception propels more of them to seek and attain such positions, thus reinforcing the notion that they are simply better leaders.

Women's Lack of Access to Networks and Sponsors

Informal networks are a precious resource for would-be leaders, yet differences in men's and women's organizational roles and career prospects, along with their proclivity to interact with others of the same gender, result in weaker networks for women. They cite as a major barrier to advancement their lack of access to influential colleagues. Moreover, the connections women do have tend to be less efficacious: Men's networks provide more informal help than women's do, and men are more likely to have mentors who help them get promoted. Meanwhile, men in positions of power tend to direct developmental opportunities to junior men, whom they view as more likely than women to succeed.

Double Binds

In most cultures masculinity and leadership are closely linked: The ideal leader, like the ideal man, is decisive, assertive, and independent. In contrast, women are expected to be nice, caretaking, and unselfish. The mismatch between conventionally feminine qualities and the qualities thought necessary for leadership puts female leaders in a double bind. Numerous studies have shown that women who excel in traditionally male domains are viewed as competent but less likable than their male counterparts. Behaviors that suggest self-confidence or assertiveness in men often appear arrogant or abrasive in women. Meanwhile, women in positions of authority who enact a conventionally feminine style may be liked but are not respected. They are deemed too emotional to make tough decisions and too soft to be strong leaders.

We find that when women recognize the subtle and pervasive effects of second-generation bias, they feel empowered, not victimized, because they can take action to counter those effects. They can put themselves forward for leadership roles when they are qualified but have been overlooked. They can seek out sponsors and others to support and develop them in those roles. They can negotiate for work arrangements that fit both their lives and their organizations' performance requirements. Such understanding makes it easier for women to "lean in."

For women and men

Second-generation bias is embedded in stereotypes and organizational practices that can be hard to detect, but when people are made aware of it, they see possibilities for change. In our work with leadership development programs, we focus on a "small wins" approach to change. In one manufacturing company, a task force learned that leaders tended to hire and promote people, mainly men, whose backgrounds and careers resembled their own. They had good reasons for this behavior: Experienced engineers were hard to find, and time constraints pressured leaders to fill roles quickly. But after recognizing some of the hidden costs of this practice—high turnover, difficulty attracting women to the company, and a lack of diversity to match that of customers—the company began to experiment with small wins. For example, some executives made a commitment to review the job criteria for leadership roles. One male leader said, "We write the job descriptions—the list of capabilities—for our ideal candidates. We know that the men will nominate themselves even if they don't meet all the requirements; the women would hold back. Now we look for the capabilities that are needed in the role, not some unrealistic ideal. We have hired more women in these roles, and our quality has not suffered in the least."

In another case, participants in a leadership development program noticed that men seemed to be given more strategic roles, whereas women were assigned more operational ones, signaling that they had lower potential. The participants proposed that the company provide clear criteria for developmental assignments, be transparent about how high potential was evaluated, and give direction as to what experiences best increased a person's potential. Those actions put more women in leadership roles.

Create Safe "Identity Workspaces"

In the upper tiers of organizations, women become increasingly scarce, which heightens the visibility and scrutiny of those near the top, who may become risk-averse and overly focused on details and lose their sense of purpose. (In general, people are less apt to try out unfamiliar behaviors or roles if they feel threatened.) Thus a safe space for learning, experimentation, and community is critical in leadership development programs for women.

Consider performance feedback, which is necessary for growth and advancement but full of trip wires for women. In many organizations 360-degree feedback is a basic tool for deepening self-knowledge and increasing awareness of one's impact on others—skills that are part and parcel of leadership development. But gender stereotypes may color evaluators' perceptions, subjecting women to double binds and double standards. Research has amply demonstrated that accomplished, high-potential women who are evaluated as competent managers often fail the likability test, whereas competence and likability tend to go hand in hand for similarly accomplished men. We see this phenomenon in our own research and practice. Supervisors routinely give high-performing women some version of the message "You need to trim your sharp elbows." Likewise, we find that participants in women's leadership development programs often receive high ratings on task-related dimensions, such as "exceeds goals," "acts decisively in the face of uncertainty," and "is not afraid to make decisions that may be unpopular," but low ratings on relational ones, such as "takes others' viewpoints into account" and "uses feedback to learn from her mistakes." We also frequently encounter women whose performance feedback seems contradictory: Some are told they need to "be tougher and hold people accountable" but also to "not set expectations so high," to "say no more often" but also to "be more visible," to "be more decisive" but also to "be more collaborative."

Creating a safe setting—a coaching relationship, a women's leadership program, a support group of peers—in which women can interpret these messages is critical to their leadership identity development. Companies should encourage them to build communities in which similarly positioned women can discuss their feedback, compare notes, and emotionally support one another's learning. Identifying common experiences increases women's willingness to talk openly, take risks, and be vulnerable without fearing that others will misunderstand or judge them. These connections are especially

FURTHER READING

"Who Will Lead and Who Will Follow? A Social Process of Leadership Identity Construction in Organizations," by D. Scott DeRue and Susan J. Ashford (*Academy of Management Review*, October 2010)

"Women and Leadership: Defining the Challenges," by Robin J. Ely and Deborah L. Rhode (*Handbook of Leadership Theory and Practice*, Harvard Business Press, 2010)

"Impossible Selves: Image Strategies and Identity Threat in Professional Women's Career Transitions," by Herminia Ibarra and Jenifer Petriglieri (Insead working paper, 2007)

"Negotiating in the Shadows of Organizations: Gender, Negotiation, and Change," by Deborah M. Kolb (*Ohio State Journal on Dispute Resolution*, 2013)

"Taking Gender into Account: Theory and Design for Women's Leadership Development Programs," by Robin J. Ely, Herminia Ibarra, and Deborah Kolb (*Academy of Management Learning & Education*, September 2011)

---

important when women are discussing sensitive topics such as gender bias or reflecting on their personal leadership challenges, which can easily threaten identity and prompt them to resist any critical feedback they may receive. When they are grounded in candid assessments of the cultural, organizational, and individual factors shaping them, women can construct coherent narratives about who they are and who they want to become.

The Importance of Leadership Purpose

In a recent interview with members of Hillary Clinton's press corps, a veteran reporter noted, "The story is never what she says, as much as we want it to be. The story is always how she looked when she said it." Clinton says she doesn't fight it anymore; she just focuses on getting the job done.

How women are perceived—how they dress, how they talk, their "executive presence," their capacity to "fill a room," and their leadership style—has been the focus of many efforts to get more of them to the top. Voice coaches, image consultants, public-speaking instructors, and branding experts find the demand for their services growing. The premise is that women have not been socialized to compete successfully in the world of men, so they must be taught the skills and styles their male counterparts acquire as a matter of course.

To manage the competence-likability trade-off—the seeming choice between being respected and being liked—women are taught to downplay femininity, or to soften a hard-charging style, or to try to strike a perfect balance between the two. But the time and energy spent on managing these perceptions can ultimately be self-defeating. Overinvestment in one's image diminishes the emotional and motivational resources available for larger purposes. People who focus on how others perceive them are less clear about their goals, less open to learning from failure, and less capable of self-regulation.

Anchoring in purpose enables women to redirect their attention toward shared goals and to consider who they need to be and what they need to learn in order to achieve those goals. Instead of defining themselves in relation to gender stereotypes—whether rejecting stereotypically masculine approaches because they feel inauthentic or rejecting stereotypically feminine ones for fear that they convey incompetence—female leaders can focus on behaving in ways that advance the purposes for which they stand.

Focusing on purpose can also lead women to take up activities that are critical to their success, such as networking. Connections rarely come to them as a matter of course, so they have to be proactive in developing ties; but we also find that many women avoid networking because they see it as inauthentic—as developing relationships that are merely transactional and feel too instrumental—or because it brings to mind activities (the proverbial golf game, for example) in which they have no interest or for which they have no time, given their responsibilities beyond work. Yet when they see it as a means to a larger purpose, such as developing new business to advance their vision for the company, they are more comfortable engaging in it.

Learning how to be an effective leader is like learning any complex skill: It rarely comes naturally and usually takes a lot of practice. Successful transitions into senior management roles involve shedding previously effective professional identities and developing new, more fitting ones. Yet people often feel ambivalent about leaving the comfort of roles in which they have excelled, because doing so means moving toward an uncertain outcome.

Second-generation gender bias can make these transitions more challenging for women, and focusing exclusively on acquiring new skills isn't sufficient; the learning must be accompanied by a growing sense of identity as a leader. That's why greater understanding of second-generation bias, safe spaces for leadership identity development, and encouraging women to anchor in their leadership purpose will get better results than the paths most organizations currently pursue.

Originally published in September 2013. Reprint R1309C

Women and the Vision Thing

by Herminia Ibarra and Otilia Obodaru

MANY BELIEVE THAT BIAS AGAINST women lingers in the business world, particularly when it comes to evaluating their leadership ability. Recently, we had a chance to see whether that assumption was true. In a study of thousands of 360-degree assessments collected by Insead's executive education program over the past five years, we looked at whether women actually received lower ratings than men. To our surprise, we found the opposite: As a group, women outshone men in most of the leadership dimensions measured. There was one exception, however, and it was a big one: Women scored lower on "envisioning"—the ability to recognize new opportunities and trends in the environment and develop a new strategic direction for an enterprise.

But was this weakness a perception or a reality? How much did it matter to women's ability to lead? And how could someone not perceived as visionary acquire the right capabilities? As we explored these issues with successful female executives, we arrived at another question: Was a reputation for vision even something many of them wanted to achieve?

A Brilliant Career

A leading services company CEO we'll call Anne Dumas typified in many ways the women we spoke with. The pillar of her leadership style was a principle taught to her 20 years ago by her first boss: Always stay close to the details. As she explained it: "I think strategy comes naturally from knowing your business and the forces that influence your market, clients, and suppliers—not at a high level but at a detailed level. Intermediaries kill your insight. You obviously can't monitor everything, but nothing should keep you from knowing in detail the processes on which your company runs—not supervising everything but understanding at a detailed level what is going on. Otherwise, you are hostage to people who will play politics. At best you don't have full information; at worst you're vulnerable to hidden agendas. My job is to go to the relevant detail level."

In her four years as CEO, Dumas had achieved some impressive results. She had doubled revenues and operating margins, given the company a new strategic direction, and undertaken a fundamental reorganization of the company's core processes and structures. More recently, she had turned her attention to developing her leadership team.

Yet Dumas knew she should somehow improve her communication effectiveness, particularly in her role as an executive member of her parent company's board. One challenge was her stylistic mismatch with her chairman, a broad-brush, big-picture thinker who often balked at what he perceived as excessive attention to detail. She found herself reluctant to favor "form over substance." She told us, "I always wonder what people mean when they say, 'He's not much of a manager but is a good leader.' Leader of what? You have to do things to be a leader." She went on to imply that so-called visionary behaviors might even be harmful. "We are in danger today of being mesmerized by people who play with our reptilian brain. For me, it is manipulation. I can do the storytelling too, but I refuse to play on people's emotions. If the string pulling is too obvious, I can't make myself do it."

Dumas's reluctance is not unusual. One of the biggest developmental hurdles that aspiring leaders, male and female alike, must clear is learning to sell their ideas—their vision of the future—to numerous stakeholders. Presenting an inspiring story about the future is very different from generating a brilliant strategic analysis

Idea in Brief

Women are still a minority in the top ranks of business. The reason? Their perceived lack of vision, according to Ibarra and Obodaru. In 360-degree feedback, women score relatively low on key elements of visioning—including ability to sense opportunities and threats, to set strategic direction, and to inspire constituents.

The authors' research suggests three explanations for women's low visioning scores:

- Some women don't buy into the value of being visionary.

- Some women lack the confidence to go out on a limb with an untested vision.

- Some women who develop a vision in collaboration with their teams don't get credit for having created one.

Regardless of the cause, women seeking more senior roles must be perceived as visionary leaders. They can start by understanding what "being visionary" means in practical terms—and then honing their visioning skills.

or crafting a logical implementation plan, competencies on which managers like Dumas have built their careers.

Indeed, a whole generation of women now entering the C-suite owe their success to a strong command of the technical elements of their jobs and a nose-to-the-grindstone focus on accomplishing quantifiable objectives. But as they step into bigger leadership roles—or are assessed on their potential to do so—the rules of the game change, and a different set of skills comes to the fore.

Vision Impaired

Our research drew on 360-degree evaluations of 2,816 executives from 149 countries enrolled in executive education courses at Insead. As with most 360-degree exercises, these managers filled out self-assessments and invited subordinates, peers, supervisors, and other people they dealt with in a professional context, such as suppliers and customers, to evaluate them on a set of leadership dimensions. In total 22,244 observers participated. (See the sidebar "Critical Components of Leadership" for a description of the Global Executive Leadership Inventory, or GELI.)

Idea in Practice

What "Being Visionary" Means

Being visionary is a matter of exercising three skills well:

Skill	How to exercise it
Sensing opportunities and threats in the environment	• Simplify complex situations by identifying broad-stroke patterns • Foresee events that will affect your organization • Conduct a vigorous exchange with an array of people inside and outside the organization
Setting strategic direction	• Encourage new business • Generate ideas for new strategies • Make decisions with an eye toward the big picture
Inspiring constituents	• Frame current practices as inadequate • Be open to new ways of doing things • Encourage others to look beyond limitations • Communicate new and better possibilities in clear, compelling ways

How to Strengthen Your Visioning Skills

• **Appreciate the importance of visioning.** Recognize vision as a matter of not just style but substance. It's not about meaningless vision statements but about strategic acumen and positioning your know-how.

As we looked for patterns within this data set, we focused on differences between the male and female leaders, both in terms of how they saw themselves and in terms of how the observers evaluated them. Certainly, there were plenty of data to work with, since 20% of the executives assessed and 27% of the evaluating observers were women. When analyzing the data, we controlled for the effects of the executives' age and level.

The first surprise for us, given prior published research, was that we found no evidence of a female "modesty effect." Quite the opposite: Women rated themselves significantly higher than men rated themselves on four of the 10 GELI dimensions we analyzed. And on

- **Leverage (or build) your network.** Formulating a vision demands a solid grasp of what's happening outside your group and organization. A good external network is the first line of defense against the insular thinking that can hurt your visioning ability.

- **Learn the craft.** Much of visioning can be learned the old-fashioned way: at the elbow of a master. Find role models and study how they develop and communicate strategic ideas. Then work with a coach to identify training and tools to build your capabilities.

- **Let go of old roles.** When you're very good at a needed task, the whole organization will conspire to keep you at it. For instance, even if delivering on the details has always been your ticket to advancement, it won't help you with visioning. Resist the urge to stay in the weeds.

- **Constantly communicate.** As you develop a vision, find opportunities to articulate it. Don't wait until it's perfect. Try out draft versions along the way, even after the vision has come into sharp focus. You won't be seen as a visionary unless you get the word out.

- **Step up to the plate.** A vision comes not only from the outside but also from greater self-confidence. Believe in your ability, and assume responsibility for creating a new and better future for others in your organization.

the remaining dimensions, the women and men gave themselves ratings that were about the same.

Our analyses of how leaders were rated by their male and female associates—bosses, peers, and subordinates—also challenged the common wisdom. Again based on prior research, we'd expected gender stereotypes to lower the ratings of female leaders, particularly those given by men. That was not the case. If there was a gender bias, it favored female leaders: Male observers scored female leaders significantly higher than they scored male leaders on seven dimensions, and female observers scored them significantly higher on eight. (See the exhibit "Comparing the Ratings of Male and Female Leaders.")

Critical Components of Leadership

THE GLOBAL EXECUTIVE LEADERSHIP INVENTORY (GELI) is a 360-degree feedback instrument developed at Insead's Global Leadership Center by Manfred Kets de Vries, Pierre Vrignaud, and Elizabeth Florent-Treacy. To identify significant dimensions of exemplary leadership, they interviewed more than 300 senior executives over the course of three years. The emerging questionnaire was then validated on an international sample of more than 300 senior executives and MBA students. The result, GELI, measures degrees of competency in these dimensions of global leadership, which it defines as follows[1]:

Envisioning
Articulating a compelling vision, mission, and strategy that incorporate a multicultural and diverse perspective and connect employees, shareholders, suppliers, and customers on a global scale.

Empowering
Empowering followers at all levels of the organization by delegating and sharing information.

Energizing
Energizing and motivating employees to achieve the organization's goals.

Designing and Aligning
Creating world-class organizational design and control systems and using them to align the behavior of employees with the organization's values and goals.

Rewarding and Feedback
Setting up the appropriate reward structures and giving constructive feedback.

Ratings on one dimension, however, defied this pattern. Female leaders were rated lower by their male observers (but not by women) on their capabilities in "envisioning." That deficit casts a large shadow over what would otherwise be an extremely favorable picture of female executives. The GELI instrument does not claim that the different dimensions of leadership are equal in importance, and as other research has shown, some do matter more than others to people's idea of what makes a leader. In particular, the envisioning dimension is, for most observers, a musthave capability.

Team Building

Creating team players and focusing on team effectiveness by instilling a co-operative atmosphere, promoting collaboration, and encouraging constructive conflict.

Outside Orientation

Making employees aware of outside constituencies, such as customers, suppliers, shareholders, and other interest groups, including local communities affected by the organization.

Global Mindset

Inculcating a global mentality, instilling values that act as a glue between the regional or national cultures represented in the organization.

Tenacity

Encouraging tenacity and courage in employees by setting a personal example in taking reasonable risks.

Emotional Intelligence

Fostering trust in the organization by creating—primarily by setting an example—an emotionally intelligent workforce whose members are self-aware and treat others with respect and understanding.

---

1. GELI contains two additional dimensions, life balance and resilience to stress, which we did not analyze in our study, since many observers were unable to provide evaluations on them.

Intrigued by this one apparent weakness, we looked more closely at the observers' ratings. Was a particular group responsible for bringing the envisioning scores down? Indeed one was. As shown in the exhibit "Who Says Women Aren't Visionary?" the male peers (who represented the majority of peers in our sample) rated women lower on envisioning. Interestingly, female peers did not downgrade women, contrary to the frequently heard claim that women compete rather than cooperate with one another. Our data suggest it's the men who might feel most competitive toward their female peers. Male superiors and subordinates rated male and female leaders about the same.

What It Means to Be Visionary

George H.W. Bush famously responded to the suggestion that he look up from the short-term goals of his campaign and start focusing on the longer term by saying, "Oh—the vision thing." His answer underlines vision's ambiguity. Just what do we mean when we say a person is visionary?

The distinction between management and leadership has long been recognized. Most agree that managing for continuous improvement to the status quo is different from being a force for change that compels a group to innovate and depart from routine. And if leadership is essentially about realizing change, then crafting and articulating a vision of a better future is a leadership prerequisite. No vision, no leadership.

But just as leadership is a question of what one does rather than what one is, so too is vision. It encompasses the abilities to frame the current practices as inadequate, to generate ideas for new strategies, and to communicate possibilities in inspiring ways to others. Being visionary, therefore, is not the same as being charismatic. It entails "naming" broad-stroke patterns and setting strategy based on those patterns. (See the sidebar "What Does It Mean to Have Vision?")

Visionary leaders don't answer the question "Where are we going?" simply for themselves; they make sure that those around them understand the direction as well. As they search for new paths, they conduct a vigorous exchange with an array of people inside and outside their organizations, knowing that great visions rarely emerge from solitary analysis. As "practical futurists," leaders also test new ideas pragmatically against current resources (money, people, organizational capabilities) and work with others to figure out how to realize the desired future. True strategists offer much more than the generic vision statements that companies hang on their walls; they articulate a clear point of view about what will transpire and position their organizations to respond to it. All of this adds up to a tall order for anyone in a leadership role. It's not obvious, however, why it should be a particular challenge for women.

Comparing the Ratings of Male and Female Leaders

IN THE 360-DEGREE ASSESSMENTS of participants in Insead's executive education program, female leaders received higher ratings than male leaders in most dimensions of leadership. But in one dimension—envisioning—women were rated lower than men.

	Which leaders rated themselves higher?	Which leaders did male observers rate higher?	Which leaders did females observers rate higher?
Envisioning	Neither	Men	**Women**
Empowering	Neither	Neither	Neither
Energizing	**Women**	**Women**	**Women**
Designing and aligning	**Women**	**Women**	**Women**
Rewarding and feedback	Neither	**Women**	**Women**
Team building	Neither	**Women**	**Women**
Outside orientation	**Women**	**Women**	**Women**
Global mindset	Neither	Neither	Neither
Tenacity	Neither	**Women**	**Women**
Emotional intelligence	**Women**	**Women**	**Women**

Perception or Reality?

As we sought to understand why women fail to impress with their vision, research findings from prior studies were not much help. To begin with, most attempts to compare men's and women's styles have focused on how leaders are rated by subordinates. Yet, as we all know, leaders play a key role in managing stakeholders above, across, and outside their units. Moreover, the vast majority of studies ask participants either to rate hypothetical male and female leaders or to evaluate "the majority" of male or female leaders they know, rather than the actual, specific leaders they know well. Empirical

Who Says Women Aren't Visionary?

IN 360-DEGREE ASSESSMENTS, women scored relatively low on vision, primarily because of scores given by their male peers.

How men and women were rated on vision*

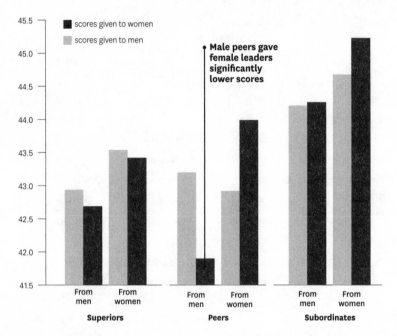

Male peers gave female leaders significantly lower scores

Superiors — Peers — Subordinates

From men / From women

*Out of a total possible score of 56. Observers ranked the leader on a scale from 1 (lowest) to 7 (highest) for eight key behaviors.

studies of gender differences in leadership styles have often used populations of students, members of diverse associations, and non-managers, rather than the midlevel to senior business managers we are actually trying to understand.

We turned therefore to the experts who were living this reality every day: the women participating in our executive education programs. When we asked how they would interpret our data, we heard three explanations. First, several women noted that they tended to set strategy via processes that differed from those used by their male counterparts. This suggests that what may in fact be visionary leadership is not perceived that way because it takes a different path. Second, we heard that women often find it risky to stray away from concrete facts, analyses, and details. And third, many women betrayed negative attitudes toward visionary leadership. Because they thought of themselves as grounded, concrete, and no-nonsense, and had seen many so-called visionary ideas founder in execution, they tended to eye envisioning behaviors with some suspicion. Each of these interpretations invited serious consideration.

Theory 1: Women are equally visionary but in a different way
Several of the women who had taken the GELI survey argued that it is not that women lack vision but that they come to their visions in a less directive way than men do. One executive put it like this: "Many women tend to be quite collaborative in forming their vision. They take into account the input of many and then describe the result as the group's vision rather than their own." Another said, "I don't see myself as particularly visionary in the creative sense. I see myself as pulling and putting together abstract pieces of information or observations that lead to possible strategies and future opportunities."

Vivienne Cox, CEO of BP Alternative Energy, is known for having an "organic" leadership style. She led a team that crafted a strategy for moving BP into alternative energy in a more unified and substantial way, by combining a set of peripheral businesses such as solar, wind, and hydrogen-fired power plants into one new low-carbon-powered unit that BP would invest billions in. Ask those involved how the new strategy came about, and the answer always involves multiple players working collaboratively. One of her key lieutenants described Cox's approach like this: "She thinks about how to create incentives or objectives so that the organization will naturally find its own solutions and structures. It encourages people to be thoughtful, innovative, and self-regulating." Cox herself claims that her role is to be a "catalyst." She consistently articulates a management philosophy in which the leader does not drive change but, rather, allows potential to emerge.

Interestingly, the processes these women describe do not hinge just on a collaborative style. They also rely on diverse and external inputs and alliances. At BP Alternative Energy, Cox spent much of her time talking to key people outside her business group and the company in order to develop a strategic perspective on opportunities and sell the idea of low-carbon power to her CEO and peers. Her ideas were informed by a wide network that included thought leaders in a range of sectors. She brought in outsiders who could transcend a parochial view to fill key roles and invited potential adversaries into the process early on to make sure her team was also informed by those who had a different view of the world. Our results hint at an interesting hypothesis: By involving their male peers in the process of creating a vision, female leaders may get less credit for the result.

Theory 2: Women hesitate to go out on a limb

Some women responded to our findings by noting that they need to base their marching orders on concrete facts and irrefutable analysis, not unprovable assertions about how the future will take shape. Here, two Democratic candidates for the 2008 U.S. presidential race offer an interesting parallel. Barack Obama was viewed as a visionary, a charismatic communicator offering a more hopeful if undetailed future. Hillary Clinton was viewed as a competent executor with an impressive if uninspiring grasp of policy detail. According to a recent *New Yorker* article by George Packer, Clinton as much as admitted that she does not inspire through rhetoric and emotion. She said: "A President, no matter how rhetorically inspiring, still has to show strength and effectiveness in the day-to-day handling of the job, because people are counting on that. So, yes, words are critically important, but they're not enough. You have to act. In my own experience, sometimes it's putting one foot in front of the other day after day."

Might women feel they have to choose between being seen as competent and in control or being visionary? Recall Anne Dumas, our services executive, and her pride in having a vast, detailed knowledge of what is happening in her firm. Often, she told us,

What Does It Mean to Have Vision?

ACROSS STUDIES AND RESEARCH TRADITIONS, vision has been found to be the central component in charismatic leadership and the essence of the oft-noted distinction between management and leadership. But what does it look like in action? As detailed by the Global Executive Leadership Inventory, behaving in a visionary way is a matter of doing three things well:

Sensing Opportunities and Threats in the Environment
- simplifying complex situations
- foreseeing events that will affect the organization

Setting Strategic Direction
- encouraging new business
- defining new strategies
- making decisions with an eye toward the big picture

Inspiring Constituents
- challenging the status quo
- being open to new ways of doing things
- inspiring others to look beyond limitations

she'd called on that reservoir of data to defend her position against challenges. The same attitude comes through in the observation of a management consultant who told us, "Men speak more confidently and boldly on an issue, with very little data to back it up. Women want to have a lot of data and feel confident that they can back up what they are saying."

A common obstacle for female leaders is that they often lack the presumption of competence accorded to their male peers. As a result, women are less likely to go out on a limb, extrapolating from facts and figures to interpretations that are more easily challenged. When a situation is rife with threat—when people, male or female, expect that they are "guilty until proven innocent"—they adopt a defensive, often rigid, posture, relying less on their imagination and creativity and sticking to safe choices.

The presumption-of-competence effect is compounded by gender stereotypes that lead us to expect emotional, collaborative women and rational, directive men. When men communicate from the heart or manage participatively, it's taken as evidence of range, an added plus. Women's emotional communication or inclusive process, by contrast, is implicitly viewed as proof of an incapacity or unwillingness to do otherwise, even if the situation calls for it.

Theory 3: Women don't put much stock in vision

Do men and women really have different leadership styles? Certainly a lot of ink has been spilled on the question, but the answer provided by hundreds of studies, subjected to meta-analysis, is no. When other factors (such as title, role, and salary) are held constant, similarities in style vastly outweigh the differences. The occasional finding that women are slightly more people oriented and participative tends not to hold up in settings where there are few women—that is, in line positions and upper management. But put aside the science and ask individuals for their opinion on whether men and women have different leadership styles, and most women (and men) answer yes.

This can only complicate the solution to the vision deficit. It's one thing for a woman who suspects she is wrongly perceived to resolve to change certain behaviors in order to convey the competence and substance she has to offer. It's quite another thing when her own self-conception has become colored by the same biases.

Our interviews with female executives highlighted one potential difference in attitude between the genders that could explain women's lower ratings on envisioning. We suspect women may not value envisioning as a critical leadership competency to the same extent that men do or may have a more skeptical view of envisioning's part in achieving results. Over and over again in our discussions with women, we heard them take pride in their concrete, no-nonsense attitude and practical orientation toward everyday work problems. We were reminded of a comment made by Margaret Thatcher: "If you want anything said, ask a man; if you want anything done, ask a woman." Many of the women we interviewed similarly expressed the opinion that women were more thorough, had a better command of detail, and were less prone to self-promotion than men. Like Anne Dumas, they valued substance over form as a means of gaining credibility with key stakeholders. A pharmaceutical executive elaborated further: "I see women as more practical. Although the women in my organization are very strategic, they are also often the ones who ground the organization in what is possible, what can or cannot be done from the human dimension."

Making the Leadership Transition

Women may dismiss the importance of vision—and they may be reassured by the many claims made over the years about their superior emotional intelligence—but the fact remains that women are a minority in the top ranks of business organizations. Our findings suggest to us that the shortfall is in no small part due to women's perceived lack of vision.

The findings of a 2008 study by Catalyst researchers Jeanine Prime and Nancy Carter and IMD professors Karsten Jonsen and Martha Maznevski concur. In it, more than 1,000 executives from nine countries (all alumni of executive education programs) were asked for their impressions of men and women in general as leaders. Both men and women tended to believe that the two genders have distinct leadership strengths, with women outscoring men on some behaviors, and men outscoring women on others. But here's the catch: When people were asked to rate the behaviors' relative importance to overall leadership effectiveness, the "male" behaviors had the edge. Across countries, "inspiring others"—a component of our envisioning dimension—landed at the top of the rankings as most important to overall leadership effectiveness. And what of the areas of leadership where men agreed that women were stronger? Let's take women's standout advantage: their much greater skill at "supporting others." That one ranked at the bottom of the list. As a component of overall leadership effectiveness, it was clearly not critical but merely nice to have.

We've seen how these priorities play out at close hand, in the personal stories of women we study. Particularly at midcareer, when senior management sizes up the leadership potential of competent managers, they take their toll. A manager we'll call Susan offers a cautionary tale. A strong performer, Susan rose through the functional ranks in logistics and distribution, thanks to her superior technical and people skills and belief in running a tight ship. As a manager she prided herself on her efficient planning and organizing and her success in building a loyal, high-performing team. But her boss saw her capabilities differently. By this point in her career, he expected her to sense emerging trends or unexploited opportunities in the business environment, to craft strategy based on a view of the business as opposed to a view of her function, and to actively work to identify and bring on board stakeholders. Eventually a proposal came from outside her division calling for a radical reorganization of it. Still focused on making continuous improvement to the existing operation, Susan lacked the networks that would have helped her spot shifting priorities in the wider market and was blindsided by the idea.

It's often observed that the very talents that bring managers success in midlevel roles can be obstacles to their taking on bigger leadership roles. That was Susan's situation, and it's possible that it is a common trap for women. Having had the message drummed into their heads that they must be rational, nonemotional, and hyperefficient, they might actually place a higher value than men on knowing the details cold and getting the job done. That, in turn, makes their leadership transition more difficult, because they stick with what they know longer. Another woman we interviewed, this one an investment banker, captured the scale of the challenge. "It's like my whole basis for existence is taken away from me," she told us, "if I can't rely on the facts." Her words reminded us that an executive's accustomed approach and style define who she is as a leader. To walk away from them is to be left without a clear sense of identity.

The challenge facing women, then, is to stop dismissing the vision thing and make vision one of the things they are known for. In a senior leadership role, it's the best use of their time and attention. It's a set of competencies that can be developed. And of all the leadership dimensions we measured, it's the only thing holding women back.

Originally published in January 2009. Reprint R0901E

The Power of Talk

Who Gets Heard and Why. *by Deborah Tannen*

THE HEAD OF A LARGE division of a multinational corporation was running a meeting devoted to performance assessment. Each senior manager stood up, reviewed the individuals in his group, and evaluated them for promotion. Although there were women in every group, not one of them made the cut. One after another, each manager declared, in effect, that every woman in his group didn't have the self-confidence needed to be promoted. The division head began to doubt his ears. How could it be that all the talented women in the division suffered from a lack of self-confidence?

In all likelihood, they didn't. Consider the many women who have left large corporations to start their own businesses, obviously exhibiting enough confidence to succeed on their own. Judgments about confidence can be inferred only from the way people present themselves, and much of that presentation is in the form of talk.

The CEO of a major corporation told me that he often has to make decisions in five minutes about matters on which others may have worked five months. He said he uses this rule: If the person making the proposal seems confident, the CEO approves it. If not, he says no. This might seem like a reasonable approach. But my field of research, sociolinguistics, suggests otherwise. The CEO obviously thinks he knows what a confident person sounds like. But his judgment, which may be dead right for some people, may be dead wrong for others.

Communication isn't as simple as saying what you mean. How you say what you mean is crucial, and differs from one person to the next, because using language is learned social behavior: How we talk and listen are deeply influenced by cultural experience. Although we might think that our ways of saying what we mean are natural, we can run into trouble if we interpret and evaluate others as if they necessarily felt the same way we'd feel if we spoke the way they did.

Since 1974, I have been researching the influence of linguistic style on conversations and human relationships. In the past four years, I have extended that research to the workplace, where I have observed how ways of speaking learned in childhood affect judgments of competence and confidence, as well as who gets heard, who gets credit, and what gets done.

The division head who was dumbfounded to hear that all the talented women in his organization lacked confidence was probably right to be skeptical. The senior managers were judging the women in their groups by their own linguistic norms, but women—like people who have grown up in a different culture—have often learned different styles of speaking than men, which can make them seem less competent and self-assured than they are.

What Is Linguistic Style?

Everything that is said must be said in a certain way—in a certain tone of voice, at a certain rate of speed, and with a certain degree of loudness. Whereas often we consciously consider what to say before speaking, we rarely think about how to say it, unless the situation is obviously loaded—for example, a job interview or a tricky performance review. Linguistic style refers to a person's characteristic speaking pattern. It includes such features as directness or indirectness, pacing and pausing, word choice, and the use of such elements as jokes, figures of speech, stories, questions, and apologies. In other words, linguistic style is a set of culturally learned signals by which we not only communicate what we mean but also interpret others' meaning and evaluate one another as people.

Consider turn taking, one element of linguistic style. Conversation is an enterprise in which people take turns: One person speaks,

Idea in Brief

Most managerial work happens through talk—discussions, meetings, presentations, negotiations. And it is through talk that managers evaluate others and are themselves judged. Using research carried out in a variety of workplace settings, linguist Deborah Tannen demonstrates how conversational style often overrides what we say, affecting who gets heard, who gets credit, and what gets done. Tannen's linguistic perspective provides managers with insight into why there is so much poor communication. Gender plays an important role. Tannen traces the ways in which women's styles can undermine them in the workplace, making them seem less competent, confident, and self-assured than they are. She analyzes the underlying social dynamic created through talk in common workplace interactions. She argues that a better understanding of linguistic style will make managers better listeners and more effective communicators, allowing them to develop more flexible approaches to a full range of managerial activities.

then the other responds. However, this apparently simple exchange requires a subtle negotiation of signals so that you know when the other person is finished and it's your turn to begin. Cultural factors such as country or region of origin and ethnic background influence how long a pause seems natural. When Bob, who is from Detroit, has a conversation with his colleague Joe, from New York City, it's hard for him to get a word in edgewise because he expects a slightly longer pause between turns than Joe does. A pause of that length never comes because, before it has a chance to, Joe senses an uncomfortable silence, which he fills with more talk of his own. Both men fail to realize that differences in conversational style are getting in their way. Bob thinks that Joe is pushy and uninterested in what he has to say, and Joe thinks that Bob doesn't have much to contribute. Similarly, when Sally relocated from Texas to Washington, D.C., she kept searching for the right time to break in during staff meetings— and never found it. Although in Texas she was considered outgoing and confident, in Washington she was perceived as shy and retiring. Her boss even suggested she take an assertiveness training course.

Idea in Practice

This table shows examples of styles of *talking* (including the *assumptions* behind each style) and *unintended consequences* a company may suffer because of misinterpreted stylistic differences.

	Style of talking	Unintended consequences of style
Sharing Credit	Uses "we" rather than "I" to describe accomplishments. *Why?* Using "I" seems too self-promoting.	Speaker doesn't get credit for accomplishments and may hesitate to offer good ideas in the future.
Acting Modest	Downplays their certainty, rather than minimizing doubts, about future performance. *Why?* Confident behavior seems too boastful.	Speaker *appears* to lack confidence and, therefore, competence; others reject speaker's good ideas.
Asking Questions	Asks questions freely. *Why?* Questions generate needed knowledge.	Speaker *appears* ignorant to others; if organization discourages speaker from asking questions, valuable knowledge remains buried.

Thus slight differences in conversational style—in these cases, a few seconds of pause—can have a surprising impact on who gets heard and on the judgments, including psychological ones, that are made about people and their abilities.

Every utterance functions on two levels. We're all familiar with the first one: Language communicates ideas. The second level is mostly invisible to us, but it plays a powerful role in communication. As a form of social behavior, language also negotiates relationships. Through ways of speaking, we signal—and create—the relative status of speakers and their level of rapport. If you say, "Sit down!" you are signaling that you have higher status than the person you are addressing, that you are so close to each other that you can

Apologizing	Apologizes freely. *Why?* Apologies express concern for others.	Speaker *appears* to lack authority.
Giving Feedback	Notes weaknesses only after *first* citing strengths. *Why?* Buffering criticism saves face for the individual receiving feedback.	Person receiving feedback concludes that areas needing improvement aren't important.
Avoiding Verbal Opposition	Avoids challenging others' ideas, and hedges when stating own ideas. *Why?* Verbal opposition signals destructive fighting.	Others conclude that speaker has weak ideas.
Managing Up	Avoids talking up achievements with higher-ups. *Why?* Emphasizing achievements to higher-ups constitutes boasting.	Managers conclude that speaker hasn't achieved much and doesn't deserve recognition or promotion.
Being Indirect	Speaks indirectly rather than bluntly when telling subordinates what to do. *Why?* Blatantly directing others is too bossy.	Subordinates conclude that manager lacks assertiveness and clear thinking, and judge manager's directives as unimportant.

drop all pleasantries, or that you are angry. If you say, "I would be honored if you would sit down," you are signaling great respect—or great sarcasm, depending on your tone of voice, the situation, and what you both know about how close you really are. If you say, "You must be so tired—why don't you sit down," you are communicating either closeness and concern or condescension. Each of these ways of saying "the same thing"—telling someone to sit down—can have a vastly different meaning.

In every community known to linguists, the patterns that constitute linguistic style are relatively different for men and women. What's "natural" for most men speaking a given language is, in some cases, different from what's "natural" for most women. That is because we learn ways of speaking as children growing up, especially from peers, and children tend to play with other children of the same sex. The research of sociologists, anthropologists, and psychologists observing American children at play has shown that, although both girls and boys find ways of creating rapport and negotiating status, girls tend to learn conversational rituals that focus on the rapport dimension of relationships whereas boys tend to learn rituals that focus on the status dimension.

Girls tend to play with a single best friend or in small groups, and they spend a lot of time talking. They use language to negotiate how close they are; for example, the girl you tell your secrets to becomes your best friend. Girls learn to downplay ways in which one is better than the others and to emphasize ways in which they are all the same. From childhood, most girls learn that sounding too sure of themselves will make them unpopular with their peers—although nobody really takes such modesty literally. A group of girls will ostracize a girl who calls attention to her own superiority and criticize her by saying, "She thinks she's something"; and a girl who tells others what to do is called "bossy." Thus girls learn to talk in ways that balance their own needs with those of others—to save face for one another in the broadest sense of the term.

Boys tend to play very differently. They usually play in larger groups in which more boys can be included, but not everyone is treated as an equal. Boys with high status in their group are expected to emphasize rather than downplay their status, and usually one or several boys will be seen as the leader or leaders. Boys generally don't accuse one another of being bossy, because the leader is expected to tell lower-status boys what to do. Boys learn to use language to negotiate their status in the group by displaying their abilities and knowledge, and by challenging others and resisting challenges. Giving orders is one way of getting and keeping the high-status role. Another is taking center stage by telling stories or jokes.

This is not to say that all boys and girls grow up this way or feel comfortable in these groups or are equally successful at negotiating within these norms. But, for the most part, these childhood play groups are where boys and girls learn their conversational styles. In this sense, they grow up in different worlds. The result is that women and men tend to have different habitual ways of saying what they mean, and conversations between them can be like cross-cultural communication: You can't assume that the other person means what you would mean if you said the same thing in the same way.

My research in companies across the United States shows that the lessons learned in childhood carry over into the workplace. Consider the following example: A focus group was organized at a major multinational company to evaluate a recently implemented flextime policy. The participants sat in a circle and discussed the new system. The group concluded that it was excellent, but they also agreed on ways to improve it. The meeting went well and was deemed a success by all, according to my own observations and everyone's comments to me. But the next day, I was in for a surprise.

I had left the meeting with the impression that Phil had been responsible for most of the suggestions adopted by the group. But as I typed up my notes, I noticed that Cheryl had made almost all those suggestions. I had thought that the key ideas came from Phil because he had picked up Cheryl's points and supported them, speaking at greater length in doing so than she had in raising them.

It would be easy to regard Phil as having stolen Cheryl's ideas—and her thunder. But that would be inaccurate. Phil never claimed Cheryl's ideas as his own. Cheryl herself told me later that she left the meeting confident that she had contributed significantly, and that she appreciated Phil's support. She volunteered, with a laugh, "It was not one of those times when a woman says something and it's ignored, then a man says it and it's picked up." In other words, Cheryl and Phil worked well as a team, the group fulfilled its charge, and the company got what it needed. So what was the problem?

I went back and asked all the participants who they thought had been the most influential group member, the one most responsible for the ideas that had been adopted. The pattern of answers was revealing. The two other women in the group named Cheryl. Two of the three men named Phil. Of the men, only Phil named Cheryl. In other words, in this instance, the women evaluated the contribution of another woman more accurately than the men did.

Meetings like this take place daily in companies around the country. Unless managers are unusually good at listening closely to how people say what they mean, the talents of someone like Cheryl may well be undervalued and underutilized.

One Up, One Down

Individual speakers vary in how sensitive they are to the social dynamics of language—in other words, to the subtle nuances of what others say to them. Men tend to be sensitive to the power dynamics of interaction, speaking in ways that position themselves as one up and resisting being put in a one-down position by others. Women tend to react more strongly to the rapport dynamic, speaking in ways that save face for others and buffering statements that could be seen as putting others in a one-down position. These linguistic patterns are pervasive; you can hear them in hundreds of exchanges in the workplace every day. And, as in the case of Cheryl and Phil, they affect who gets heard and who gets credit.

Getting credit

Even so small a linguistic strategy as the choice of pronoun can affect who gets credit. In my research in the workplace, I heard men say "I" in situations where I heard women say "we." For example, one publishing company executive said, "I'm hiring a new manager. I'm going to put him in charge of my marketing division," as if he owned the corporation. In stark contrast, I recorded women saying "we" when referring to work they alone had done. One woman explained that it would sound too self-promoting to claim credit in an obvious way by saying, "I did this." Yet she expected—sometimes vainly—that others would know it was her work and would give her the credit she did not claim for herself.

Managers might leap to the conclusion that women who do not take credit for what they've done should be taught to do so. But that solution is problematic because we associate ways of speaking with moral qualities: The way we speak is who we are and who we want to be.

Veronica, a senior researcher in a high-tech company, had an observant boss. He noticed that many of the ideas coming out of the group were hers but that often someone else trumpeted them around the office and got credit for them. He advised her to "own" her ideas and make sure she got the credit. But Veronica found she simply didn't enjoy her work if she had to approach it as what seemed to her an unattractive and unappealing "grabbing game." It was her dislike of such behavior that had led her to avoid it in the first place.

Whatever the motivation, women are less likely than men to have learned to blow their own horn. And they are more likely than men to believe that if they do so, they won't be liked.

Many have argued that the growing trend of assigning work to teams may be especially congenial to women, but it may also create complications for performance evaluation. When ideas are generated and work is accomplished in the privacy of the team, the outcome of the team's effort may become associated with the person most vocal about reporting results. There are many women and men—but probably relatively more women—who are reluctant to put themselves forward in this way and who consequently risk not getting credit for their contributions.

Confidence and boasting

The CEO who based his decisions on the confidence level of speakers was articulating a value that is widely shared in U.S. businesses: One way to judge confidence is by an individual's behavior, especially verbal behavior. Here again, many women are at a disadvantage.

Studies show that women are more likely to downplay their certainty and men are more likely to minimize their doubts. Psychologist Laurie Heatherington and her colleagues devised an ingenious experiment, which they reported in the journal *Sex Roles* (Volume 29, 1993). They asked hundreds of incoming college students to predict what grades they would get in their first year. Some subjects were asked to make their predictions privately by writing them down and placing them in an envelope; others were asked to make their predictions publicly, in the presence of a researcher. The results showed that more women than men predicted lower grades for themselves if they made their predictions publicly. If they made their predictions privately, the predictions were the same as those of the men—and the same as their actual grades. This study provides evidence that what comes across as lack of confidence—predicting lower grades for oneself—may reflect not one's actual level of confidence but the desire not to seem boastful.

These habits with regard to appearing humble or confident result from the socialization of boys and girls by their peers in childhood play. As adults, both women and men find these behaviors reinforced by the positive responses they get from friends and relatives who share the same norms. But the norms of behavior in the U.S. business world are based on the style of interaction that is more common among men—at least, among American men.

Asking questions

Although asking the right questions is one of the hallmarks of a good manager, how and when questions are asked can send unintended signals about competence and power. In a group, if only one person asks questions, he or she risks being seen as the only ignorant one. Furthermore, we judge others not only by how they speak but also by how they are spoken to. The person who asks questions may end up being lectured to and looking like a novice under a schoolmaster's tutelage. The way boys are socialized makes them more likely to be aware of the underlying power dynamic by which a question asker can be seen in a one-down position.

One practicing physician learned the hard way that any exchange of information can become the basis for judgments—or misjudgments—about competence. During her training, she received a negative evaluation that she thought was unfair, so she asked her supervising physician for an explanation. He said that she knew less than her peers. Amazed at his answer, she asked how he had reached that conclusion. He said, "You ask more questions."

Along with cultural influences and individual personality, gender seems to play a role in whether and when people ask questions. For example, of all the observations I've made in lectures and books, the one that sparks the most enthusiastic flash of recognition is that men are less likely than women to stop and ask for directions when they are lost. I explain that men often resist asking for directions because they are aware that it puts them in a one-down position and because they value the independence that comes with finding their way by themselves. Asking for directions while driving is only one instance—along with many others that researchers have examined—in which men seem less likely than women to ask questions. I believe this is because they are more attuned than women to the potential face-losing aspect of asking questions. And men who believe that asking questions might reflect negatively on them may, in turn, be likely to form a negative opinion of others who ask questions in situations where they would not.

Conversational Rituals

Conversation is fundamentally ritual in the sense that we speak in ways our culture has conventionalized and expect certain types of responses. Take greetings, for example. I have heard visitors to the United States complain that Americans are hypocritical because they ask how you are but aren't interested in the answer. To Americans, How are you? is obviously a ritualized way to start a conversation rather than a literal request for information. In other parts of the world, including the Philippines, people ask each other, "Where are you going?" when they meet. The question seems intrusive to Americans, who do not realize that it, too, is a ritual query to which the only expected reply is a vague "Over there."

It's easy and entertaining to observe different rituals in foreign countries. But we don't expect differences, and are far less likely to recognize the ritualized nature of our conversations, when we are with our compatriots at work. Our differing rituals can be even more problematic when we think we're all speaking the same language.

Apologies

Consider the simple phrase *I'm sorry*.

Catherine: How did that big presentation go?

Bob: Oh, not very well. I got a lot of flak from the VP for finance, and I didn't have the numbers at my fingertips.

Catherine: Oh, I'm sorry. I know how hard you worked on that.

In this case, *I'm sorry* probably means "I'm sorry that happened," not "I apologize," unless it was Catherine's responsibility to supply Bob with the numbers for the presentation. Women tend to say *I'm sorry* more frequently than men, and often they intend it in this way—as a ritualized means of expressing concern. It's one of many learned elements of conversational style that girls often use to establish rapport. Ritual apologies—like other conversational rituals—work well when both parties share the same assumptions about their use. But people who utter frequent ritual apologies may end up appearing weaker, less confident, and literally more blameworthy than people who don't.

Apologies tend to be regarded differently by men, who are more likely to focus on the status implications of exchanges. Many men avoid apologies because they see them as putting the speaker in a one-down position. I observed with some amazement an encounter among several lawyers engaged in a negotiation over a speakerphone. At one point, the lawyer in whose office I was sitting accidentally elbowed the telephone and cut off the call. When his secretary got the parties back on again, I expected him to say what I would have said: "Sorry about that. I knocked the phone with my elbow." Instead, he said, "Hey, what happened? One minute you were there; the next minute you were gone!" This lawyer seemed to have an automatic impulse not to admit fault if he didn't have to. For me, it was one of those pivotal moments when you realize that the world you live in is not the one everyone lives in and that the way you assume is the way to talk is really only one of many.

Those who caution managers not to undermine their authority by apologizing are approaching interaction from the perspective of the power dynamic. In many cases, this strategy is effective. On the other hand, when I asked people what frustrated them in their jobs, one frequently voiced complaint was working with or for someone who refuses to apologize or admit fault. In other words, accepting responsibility for errors and admitting mistakes may be an equally effective or superior strategy in some settings.

Feedback

Styles of giving feedback contain a ritual element that often is the cause for misunderstanding. Consider the following exchange: A manager had to tell her marketing director to rewrite a report. She began this potentially awkward task by citing the report's strengths and then moved to the main point: the weaknesses that needed to be remedied. The marketing director seemed to understand and accept his supervisor's comments, but his revision contained only minor changes and failed to address the major weaknesses. When the manager told him of her dissatisfaction, he accused her of misleading him: "You told me it was fine."

The impasse resulted from different linguistic styles. To the manager, it was natural to buffer the criticism by beginning with praise. Telling her subordinate that his report is inadequate and has to be rewritten puts him in a one-down position. Praising him for the parts that are good is a ritualized way of saving face for him. But the marketing director did not share his supervisor's assumption about how feedback should be given. Instead, he assumed that what she mentioned first was the main point and that what she brought up later was an afterthought.

Those who expect feedback to come in the way the manager presented it would appreciate her tact and would regard a more blunt approach as unnecessarily callous. But those who share the marketing director's assumptions would regard the blunt approach as honest and no-nonsense, and the manager's as obfuscating. Because each one's assumptions seemed self-evident, each blamed the other: The manager thought the marketing director was not listening, and he thought she had not communicated clearly or had changed her mind. This is significant because it illustrates that incidents labeled vaguely as "poor communication" may be the result of differing linguistic styles.

Compliments

Exchanging compliments is a common ritual, especially among women. A mismatch in expectations about this ritual left Susan, a manager in the human resources field, in a one-down position. She and her colleague Bill had both given presentations at a national conference. On the airplane home, Susan told Bill, "That was a great talk!" "Thank you," he said. Then she asked, "What did you think of mine?" He responded with a lengthy and detailed critique, as she listened uncomfortably. An unpleasant feeling of having been put down came over her. Somehow she had been positioned as the novice in need of his expert advice. Even worse, she had only herself to blame, since she had, after all, asked Bill what he thought of her talk.

But had Susan asked for the response she received? When she asked Bill what he thought about her talk, she expected to hear not a critique but a compliment. In fact, her question had been an attempt to repair a ritual gone awry. Susan's initial compliment to Bill was the kind of automatic recognition she felt was more or less required after a colleague gives a presentation, and she expected Bill to respond with a matching compliment. She was just talking automatically, but he either sincerely misunderstood the ritual or simply took the opportunity to bask in the one-up position of critic. Whatever his motivation, it was Susan's attempt to spark an exchange of compliments that gave him the opening.

Although this exchange could have occurred between two men, it does not seem coincidental that it happened between a man and a woman. Linguist Janet Holmes discovered that women pay more compliments than men (*Anthropological Linguistics,* Volume 28, 1986). And, as I have observed, fewer men are likely to ask, "What did you think of my talk?" precisely because the question might invite an unwanted critique.

In the social structure of the peer groups in which they grow up, boys are indeed looking for opportunities to put others down and take the one-up position for themselves. In contrast, one of the rituals girls learn is taking the one-down position but assuming that the other person will recognize the ritual nature of the self-denigration and pull them back up.

The exchange between Susan and Bill also suggests how women's and men's characteristic styles may put women at a disadvantage in the workplace. If one person is trying to minimize status differences, maintain an appearance that everyone is equal, and save face for the other, while another person is trying to maintain the one-up position and avoid being positioned as one down, the person seeking the one-up position is likely to get it. At the same time, the person who has not been expending any effort to avoid the one-down position is likely to end up in it. Because women are more likely to take (or accept) the role of advice seeker, men are more inclined to interpret a ritual question from a woman as a request for advice.

Ritual opposition

Apologizing, mitigating criticism with praise, and exchanging compliments are rituals common among women that men often take literally. A ritual common among men that women often take literally is ritual opposition.

A woman in communications told me she watched with distaste and distress as her office mate argued heatedly with another colleague about whose division should suffer budget cuts. She was even more surprised, however, that a short time later they were as friendly as ever. "How can you pretend that fight never happened?" she asked. "Who's pretending it never happened?" he responded, as puzzled by her question as she had been by his behavior. "It happened," he said, "and it's over." What she took as literal fighting to him was a routine part of daily negotiation: a ritual fight.

Many Americans expect the discussion of ideas to be a ritual fight—that is, an exploration through verbal opposition. They present their own ideas in the most certain and absolute form they can, and wait to see if they are challenged. Being forced to defend an idea provides an opportunity to test it. In the same spirit, they may play devil's advocate in challenging their colleagues' ideas—trying to poke holes and find weaknesses—as a way of helping them explore and test their ideas.

This style can work well if everyone shares it, but those unaccustomed to it are likely to miss its ritual nature. They may give up an idea that is challenged, taking the objections as an indication that the idea was a poor one. Worse, they may take the opposition as a personal attack and may find it impossible to do their best in a contentious environment. People unaccustomed to this style may hedge when stating their ideas in order to fend off potential attacks. Ironically, this posture makes their arguments appear weak and is more likely to invite attack from pugnacious colleagues than to fend it off.

Ritual opposition can even play a role in who gets hired. Some consulting firms that recruit graduates from the top business schools use a confrontational interviewing technique. They challenge the candidate to "crack a case" in real time. A partner at one firm told me, "Women tend to do less well in this kind of interaction, and it certainly affects who gets hired. But, in fact, many women who don't 'test well' turn out to be good consultants. They're often smarter than some of the men who looked like analytic powerhouses under pressure."

The level of verbal opposition varies from one company's culture to the next, but I saw instances of it in all the organizations I studied. Anyone who is uncomfortable with this linguistic style—and that includes some men as well as many women—risks appearing insecure about his or her ideas.

Negotiating Authority

In organizations, formal authority comes from the position one holds. But actual authority has to be negotiated day to day. The effectiveness of individual managers depends in part on their skill in negotiating authority and on whether others reinforce or undercut their efforts. The way linguistic style reflects status plays a subtle role in placing individuals within a hierarchy.

Managing up and down

In all the companies I researched, I heard from women who knew they were doing a superior job and knew that their coworkers (and sometimes their immediate bosses) knew it as well, but believed that the higher-ups did not. They frequently told me that something outside themselves was holding them back and found it frustrating because they thought that all that should be necessary for success was to do a great job, that superior performance should be recognized and rewarded. In contrast, men often told me that if women weren't promoted, it was because they simply weren't up to snuff. Looking around, however, I saw evidence that men more often than women behaved in ways likely to get them recognized by those with the power to determine their advancement.

In all the companies I visited, I observed what happened at lunchtime. I saw young men who regularly ate lunch with their boss, and senior men who ate with the big boss. I noticed far fewer women who sought out the highest-level person they could eat with. But one is more likely to get recognition for work done if one talks about it to those higher up, and it is easier to do so if the lines of communication are already open. Furthermore, given the opportunity for a conversation with superiors, men and women are likely to have different ways of talking about their accomplishments because of the different ways in which they were socialized as children. Boys are rewarded by their peers if they talk up their achievements, whereas girls are rewarded if they play theirs down. Linguistic styles common among men may tend to give them some advantages when it comes to managing up.

All speakers are aware of the status of the person they are talking to and adjust accordingly. Everyone speaks differently when talking to a boss than when talking to a subordinate. But, surprisingly, the ways in which they adjust their talk may be different and thus may project different images of themselves.

Communications researchers Karen Tracy and Eric Eisenberg studied how relative status affects the way people give criticism. They devised a business letter that contained some errors and asked

13 male and 11 female college students to role-play delivering criticism under two scenarios. In the first, the speaker was a boss talking to a subordinate; in the second, the speaker was a subordinate talking to his or her boss. The researchers measured how hard the speakers tried to avoid hurting the feelings of the person they were criticizing.

One might expect people to be more careful about how they deliver criticism when they are in a subordinate position. Tracy and Eisenberg found that hypothesis to be true for the men in their study but not for the women. As they reported in *Research on Language and Social Interaction* (Volume 24, 1990/1991), the women showed more concern about the other person's feelings when they were playing the role of superior. In other words, the women were more careful to save face for the other person when they were managing down than when they were managing up. This pattern recalls the way girls are socialized: Those who are in some way superior are expected to downplay rather than flaunt their superiority.

In my own recordings of workplace communication, I observed women talking in similar ways. For example, when a manager had to correct a mistake made by her secretary, she did so by acknowledging that there were mitigating circumstances. She said, laughing, "You know, it's hard to do things around here, isn't it, with all these people coming in!" The manager was saving face for her subordinate, just like the female students role-playing in the Tracy and Eisenberg study.

Is this an effective way to communicate? One must ask, effective for what? The manager in question established a positive environment in her group, and the work was done effectively. On the other hand, numerous women in many different fields told me that their bosses say they don't project the proper authority.

Indirectness

Another linguistic signal that varies with power and status is indirectness—the tendency to say what we mean without spelling it out in so many words. Despite the widespread belief in the United

States that it's always best to say exactly what we mean, indirectness is a fundamental and pervasive element in human communication. It also is one of the elements that vary most from one culture to another, and it can cause enormous misunderstanding when speakers have different habits and expectations about how it is used. It's often said that American women are more indirect than American men, but in fact everyone tends to be indirect in some situations and in different ways. Allowing for cultural, ethnic, regional, and individual differences, women are especially likely to be indirect when it comes to telling others what to do, which is not surprising, considering girls' readiness to brand other girls as bossy. On the other hand, men are especially likely to be indirect when it comes to admitting fault or weakness, which also is not surprising, considering boys' readiness to push around boys who assume the one-down position.

At first glance, it would seem that only the powerful can get away with bald commands such as, "Have that report on my desk by noon." But power in an organization also can lead to requests so indirect that they don't sound like requests at all. A boss who says, "Do we have the sales data by product line for each region?" would be surprised and frustrated if a subordinate responded, "We probably do" rather than "I'll get it for you."

Examples such as these notwithstanding, many researchers have claimed that those in subordinate positions are more likely to speak indirectly, and that is surely accurate in some situations. For example, linguist Charlotte Linde, in a study published in *Language in Society* (Volume 17, 1988), examined the black-box conversations that took place between pilots and copilots before airplane crashes. In one particularly tragic instance, an Air Florida plane crashed into the Potomac River immediately after attempting takeoff from National Airport in Washington, D.C., killing all but 5 of the 74 people on board. The pilot, it turned out, had little experience flying in icy weather. The copilot had a bit more, and it became heartbreakingly clear on analysis that he had tried to warn the pilot but had done so indirectly. Alerted by Linde's observation, I examined the transcript of the conversations and found evidence of her hypothesis.

The copilot repeatedly called attention to the bad weather and to ice buildup on other planes:

> *Copilot:* Look how the ice is just hanging on his, ah, back, back there, see that? See all those icicles on the back there and everything?
>
> *Pilot:* Yeah.
>
> [The copilot also expressed concern about the long waiting time since deicing.]
>
> *Copilot:* Boy, this is a, this is a losing battle here on trying to deice those things; it [gives] you a false feeling of security, that's all that does.
>
> [Just before they took off, the copilot expressed another concern—about abnormal instrument readings—but again he didn't press the matter when it wasn't picked up by the pilot.]
>
> *Copilot:* That don't seem right, does it? [3-second pause]. Ah, that's not right. Well—
>
> *Pilot:* Yes it is, there's 80.
>
> *Copilot:* Naw, I don't think that's right. [7-second pause] Ah, maybe it is.

Shortly thereafter, the plane took off, with tragic results. In other instances as well as this one, Linde observed that copilots, who are second in command, are more likely to express themselves indirectly or otherwise mitigate, or soften, their communication when they are suggesting courses of action to the pilot. In an effort to avert similar disasters, some airlines now offer training for copilots to express themselves in more assertive ways.

This solution seems self-evidently appropriate to most Americans. But when I assigned Linde's article in a graduate seminar I taught, a Japanese student pointed out that it would be just as effective to train pilots to pick up on hints. This approach reflects assumptions about communication that typify Japanese culture, which places great value on the ability of people to understand one another without putting everything into words. Either directness or indirectness can be a successful means of communication as long as the linguistic style is understood by the participants.

In the world of work, however, there is more at stake than whether the communication is understood. People in powerful positions are likely to reward styles similar to their own, because we all tend to take as self-evident the logic of our own styles. Accordingly, there is evidence that in the U.S. workplace, where instructions from a superior are expected to be voiced in a relatively direct manner, those who tend to be indirect when telling subordinates what to do may be perceived as lacking in confidence.

Consider the case of the manager at a national magazine who was responsible for giving assignments to reporters. She tended to phrase her assignments as questions. For example, she asked, "How would you like to do the X project with Y?" or said, "I was thinking of putting you on the X project. Is that okay?" This worked extremely well with her staff; they liked working for her, and the work got done in an efficient and orderly manner. But when she had her midyear evaluation with her own boss, he criticized her for not assuming the proper demeanor with her staff.

In any work environment, the higher-ranking person has the power to enforce his or her view of appropriate demeanor, created in part by linguistic style. In most U.S. contexts, that view is likely to assume that the person in authority has the right to be relatively direct rather than to mitigate orders. There also are cases, however, in which the higher-ranking person assumes a more indirect style. The owner of a retail operation told her subordinate, a store manager, to do something. He said he would do it, but a week later he still hadn't. They were able to trace the difficulty to the following conversation: She had said, "The bookkeeper needs help with the billing. How would you feel about helping her out?" He had said, "Fine." This conversation had seemed to be clear and flawless at the time, but it turned out that they had interpreted this simple exchange in very different ways. She thought he meant, "Fine, I'll help the bookkeeper out." He thought he meant, "Fine, I'll think about how I would feel about helping the bookkeeper out." He did think about it and came to the conclusion that he had more important things to do and couldn't spare the time.

To the owner, "How would you feel about helping the bookkeeper out?" was an obviously appropriate way to give the order "Help the bookkeeper out with the billing." Those who expect orders to be given as bald imperatives may find such locutions annoying or even misleading. But those for whom this style is natural do not think they are being indirect. They believe they are being clear in a polite or respectful way.

What is atypical in this example is that the person with the more indirect style was the boss, so the store manager was motivated to adapt to her style. She still gives orders the same way, but the store manager now understands how she means what she says. It's more common in U.S. business contexts for the highest-ranking people to take a more direct style, with the result that many women in authority risk being judged by their superiors as lacking the appropriate demeanor—and, consequently, lacking confidence.

What to Do?

I am often asked, What is the best way to give criticism? or What is the best way to give orders?—in other words, What is the best way to communicate? The answer is that there is no one best way. The results of a given way of speaking will vary depending on the situation, the culture of the company, the relative rank of speakers, their linguistic styles, and how those styles interact with one another. Because of all those influences, any way of speaking could be perfect for communicating with one person in one situation and disastrous with someone else in another. The critical skill for managers is to become aware of the workings and power of linguistic style, to make sure that people with something valuable to contribute get heard.

It may seem, for example, that running a meeting in an unstructured way gives equal opportunity to all. But awareness of the differences in conversational style makes it easy to see the potential for unequal access. Those who are comfortable speaking up in groups, who need little or no silence before raising their hands, or who speak out easily without waiting to be recognized are far more likely to get heard at meetings. Those who refrain from talking until it's clear that the previous speaker is finished, who wait to be recognized, and who are inclined to link their comments to those of others will do fine at a meeting where everyone else is following the same rules but will have a hard time getting heard in a meeting with people whose styles are more like the first pattern. Given the socialization typical of boys and girls, men are more likely to have learned the first style and women the second, making meetings more congenial for men than for women. It's common to observe women who participate actively in one-on-one discussions or in all-female groups but who are seldom heard in meetings with a large proportion of men. On the other hand, there are women who share the style more common among men, and they run a different risk—of being seen as too aggressive.

A manager aware of those dynamics might devise any number of ways of ensuring that everyone's ideas are heard and credited. Although no single solution will fit all contexts, managers who understand the dynamics of linguistic style can develop more adaptive and flexible approaches to running or participating in meetings, mentoring or advancing the careers of others, evaluating performance, and so on. Talk is the lifeblood of managerial work, and understanding that different people have different ways of saying what they mean will make it possible to take advantage of the talents of people with a broad range of linguistic styles. As the workplace becomes more culturally diverse and business becomes more global, managers will need to become even better at reading interactions and more flexible in adjusting their own styles to the people with whom they interact.

Originally published in September–October 1995. Reprint 95510
Adapted from *Talking from 9 to 5: How Women's and Men's Conversation Styles Affect Who Gets Heard, Who Gets Credit, and What Gets Done at Work* by Deborah Tannen (New York: Avon Books, 1995).

The Memo Every Woman Keeps in Her Desk

by Kathleen Reardon

Author's note: *When I wrote "The Memo Every Woman Keeps in Her Desk" in 1993 it was generally thought that men rising in the workforce at that time would be far more comfortable working beside women than their fathers had been.*

I wrote the case study to reflect what I saw at the time—that women directly competing with men for jobs was easier to accept in theory than in reality, especially at senior levels. And while it wasn't acceptable in most organizations to overtly voice objections to women's promotions simply because of gender, that did not mean such feelings no longer existed. With regard to gender equity, the job was far from done in 1993 and remains far from done now.

Of course, there have been many positive changes in the last twenty-five years. The overall pay gap has narrowed somewhat. Increasingly, there are efforts to recruit women to the fields of science, math, and engineering. Women are seeking graduate degrees in higher numbers than ever before and are very well represented among successful entrepreneurs.

But despite these and other positive changes, the memo case has stayed surprisingly relevant. It did not focus on sexual harassment or assault but rather on a young woman's intention to inform her CEO of an atmosphere in their workplace that slowly eroded a "woman's sense of worth and place." The case posed several questions still faced today. Should a woman tell her CEO about issues creating a hostile work culture for her and other female employees? Should she do so alone? What is the right way to word and convey such a message? What are the risks? Is it likely that a male CEO will listen and appreciate such unsolicited input?

In the light of the #MeToo movement, a woman's decision to speak up may seem less risky now, especially about issues relatively low on the spectrum of gender-based offenses. But is that the case? Or do we still have a long way to go before women can share their experiences with confidence that their observations and courage will not only be welcomed but lead to significant change?

—Kathleen Reardon, January 2018

Editor's note: *The following is a fictionalized case study that appeared in* Harvard Business Review *along with commentary from experts.*

What kind of advice was I going to give Liz Ames, my pal from the good old days when we worked together in market development at Vision Software? Liz and I had been through a lot together, from working for an egomaniac who was finally fired to laying the groundwork for the biggest product launch in the company's history. We always seemed to understand each other's thoughts, and those Friday nights unwinding at the tavern made it possible for both of us to face work again Monday morning. We both had come a long way at Vision, and we were genuinely glad to see the other succeed. When I got the marketing director position in Germany, Liz was the first to congratulate me.

When we met for dinner the first night of the annual marketing retreat, I was ready to tell Liz all about my first six months on the new job, but she made it clear from the start that she had something urgent to discuss. She needed me to help her out of a dilemma, and she said my perspective as a man would be helpful. She had written a memo to John Clark, Vision's CEO, complaining about sexism at the company. Now she was agonizing over whether to send it. Liz seldom raised the subject of sexism, but she had written the memo because she thought it was time that someone at the top knew what was really going on at the company—in the trenches, as she put it.

She had no doubt that the message was important. But she did have doubts about how it would be received and about the fate of the messenger. She wanted me, her most trusted friend at Vision and a man, to help her decide what to do.

"In an ideal world," she said, "I wouldn't have any second thoughts about sending it. But you know what can happen to messengers. If Clark likes what I have to say, there's no problem. But then, there are the other possibilities."

"You've never been afraid to speak your mind. What's the worst that could happen?" I asked.

"Clark isn't going to fire me, if that's what you mean. But I can think of several ways this thing could backfire. What if Clark doesn't believe me, or he just can't relate to what I'm saying? He'll dismiss me as a radical feminist or a chronic complainer. Word will get around, and my career at Vision will be over. Or maybe he won't respond at all. It'll be one more example of not being heard. I don't know if I have the mental energy for that."

At first I thought Liz was being melodramatic, but as we talked I could see that to her, the decision was a turning point. She knew that ultimately she had to take responsibility for whatever decision she made, but she wanted my perspective. Reluctantly, I promised to use the memo as bedtime reading and get back to her in the morning. So there I sat with the memo in my lap, the hotel lamp glaring off the neatly typed pages.

Liz's memo seemed reasonable and compelling. Wouldn't Clark be grateful to hear from someone in the trenches? He liked to boast about the company's progressive policies toward diversity, and this would give him a chance to renew the crusade. He'd respect Liz for taking his commitment seriously.

But then again, Clark had an ego. Maybe he'd resent the implication that the company is not what he professes it to be. And, of course, it wasn't John Clark whom Liz had to face every day. Not all of Liz's male colleagues would give her criticisms any credence. And if they heard that she was writing to the boss complaining about them, they would shut her out. I had to admit, I could imagine that happening.

To: Mr. John Clark, CEO
From: Elizabeth C. Ames,
Director of Consumer Marketing
Date: March 8, 1993

I've been working in the marketing department at Vision Software for more than ten years, where I've had my share of challenges and successes. I've enjoyed being part of an interesting and exciting company. Despite my general enthusiasm about the company and my job, however, I was taken aback when I received your memo announcing the resignations of Mariam Blackwell and Susan French, Vision's two most senior women. This is not the first time Vision has lost its highest ranking women. Just nine months ago, Kathryn Hobbs resigned, and a year before that, it was Suzanne LaHaise. The reasons are surprisingly similar: they wanted to "spend more time with their families" or "explore new career directions."

I can't help but detect a disturbing pattern. Why do such capable, conscientious women who have demonstrated intense commitment to their careers suddenly want to change course or spend more time at home? It's a question I've thought long and hard about.

Despite Vision's policies to hire and promote women and your own efforts to recognize and reward women's contributions, the overall atmosphere in this company is one that slowly erodes a woman's sense of worth and place. I believe that top-level women are leaving Vision Software not because they are drawn to other pursuits but because they are tired of struggling against a climate of female failure. Little things that happen daily—things many men don't even notice and women can't help but notice—send subtle messages that women are less important, less talented, less likely to make a difference than their male peers.

Let me try to describe what I mean. I'll start with meetings, which are a way of life at Vision and one of the most devaluing experiences for women. Women are often talked over and interrupted; their ideas never seem to be heard. Last week, I attended a meeting with ten men and one other woman. As soon as the woman started her presentation, several side conversations began. Her presentation skills were excellent, but she couldn't seem to get people's attention. When it was time to take questions, one man said dismissively,

Did the consequences of sending the memo really matter? Wasn't there a principle involved? I knew that the stonewalling Liz had referred to was real. I'd witnessed it myself over the years. Liz was

"We did something like this a couple of years ago, and it didn't work." She explained how her ideas differed, but the explanation fell on deaf ears. When I tried to give her support by expressing interest, I was interrupted.

But it's not just meetings. There are many things that make women feel unwelcome or unimportant. One department holds its biannual retreats at a country club with a "men only" bar. At the end of the sessions, the men typically hang around at the bar and talk, while the women quietly disappear. Needless to say, important information is often shared during those casual conversations.

Almost every formal meeting is followed by a series of informal ones behind closed doors. Women are rarely invited. Nor are they privy to the discussions before the formal meetings. As a result, they are often less likely to know what the boss has on his mind and therefore less prepared to react.

My female colleagues and I are also subjected to a daily barrage of seemingly innocent comments that belittle women. A coworker of mine recently boasted about how much he respects women by saying, "My wife is the wind beneath my wings. In fact, some people call me Mr. Karen Snyder." The men chuckled; the women didn't. And just last week, a male colleague stood up at 5:30 and jokingly informed a group of us that he would be leaving early: "I have to play mom tonight." Women play mom every night, and it never gets a laugh. In fact, most women try to appear devoid of concern about their families.

Any one of these incidents on its own is a small thing. But together and in repetition, they are quite powerful. The women at Vision fight to get their ideas heard and to crack the informal channels of information. Their energy goes into keeping up, not getting ahead, until they just don't have any more to give.

I can assure you that my observations are shared by many women in the company. I can only speculate that they were shared by Mariam Blackwell and Susan French.

Vision needs men *and* women if it is to become the preeminent educational software company. We need to send stronger, clearer signals that men are not the only people who matter. And this kind of change can work only if it starts with strong commitment at the top. That's why I'm writing to you. If I can be of help, please let me know.

one of the most positive and energetic people I knew, but I remember several times when she was so strung out from having to prove herself to men who constantly challenged her authority that she was ready to quit. That would have been a serious loss of experience. She knew how to work with educators better than anyone I knew, and her impeccable follow-up was largely responsible for the success of the Vision II product line that now represents 20% of Vision's revenues.

But men were under pressure too. Maybe it just took a different form. Vision was a tough place, and marketing was the toughest department. Many times, I was tempted to pack it in myself. I'd seen a lot of men fail and a lot of women succeed at Vision. Take Mariam Blackwell. She fit Vision's corporate culture like a glove. If she wasn't heard the first time, she'd say it again. I think she left because she ran out of challenges, not because her psychic energy had been depleted. Susan French left because they gave her a V.P. title but removed the decision-making authority of her male predecessors— something Liz had not mentioned in her memo.

As I wrestled with the issues Liz raised, I realized that her dilemma had become a dilemma for me. If I advised Liz to send the memo, was I being naive about the consequences she might suffer? If I told her not to send it, was I somehow condoning the behavior she described? If I suggested that women were not the only ones who were sometimes run aground by Vision's demanding environment, was I being insensitive? If I don't buy into it, does that mean that I just don't get it?

What would I tell Liz?

Should Liz Send the Memo?

Richard D. Glovsky is the former chief of the Civil Division of the United States Attorney's Office in Boston. He is the founder of Boston-based Glovsky & Associates, a law firm that specializes in employment law.

I would advise Liz not to send the memo at this time. A vigilant CEO would not have permitted this kind of discriminatory work environment to evolve in the first place. In short, the issues with which Liz is concerned would not exist at Vision unless Clark tacitly allowed them to develop. Clark cannot be trusted with Liz's message.

Instead of sending it, Liz should marshal her resources. She should speak with Mariam Blackwell, Susan French, Kathryn Hobbs, and Suzanne LaHaise to ascertain whether they have similar observations and would support her publicly. Liz also should talk to other women at Vision who can be trusted to maintain her confidence.

She should not "go it alone," especially when addressing a man more likely to be unreceptive than sympathetic. If Liz can get support (and statements) from other women who will corroborate her claims, she may be able to force Clark to do what is proper: review the employment environment at Vision and address Liz's issues on a companywide basis.

Finally, if Liz decides to take her message to Clark, she should either see him in person with as many other credible colleagues she can collect or send a memo signed by several Vision employees.

At a meeting, she should not be the only person to speak. Liz and her colleagues should divide the presentation so that no one person is the messenger. Clark will have a tendency to be vengeful and will focus on the leader of the group.

Unfortunately, because Clark may not react positively to the memo, Liz must use a more calculated and broad-based approach.

Philip A. Marineau is executive vice president and chief operating officer at the Quaker Oats Company, Chicago, Illinois.
My advice is to send the memo. Sure, it's a risk. But not sending it will lead only to greater frustration—and eventually Liz will resign anyway. Chances are the CEO is already alarmed about the loss of his top two women executives and is wondering what he can do to prevent others from leaving. If he's smart, he'll not only listen to Liz's concerns but also make her a part of the search for solutions.

It's been my experience that listening to bright, committed employees throughout the company—regardless of gender, race, or level of experience—is one of the most important aspects of my job. It's the best way for me to identify situations that need more resources or attention from management.

Working with Quaker's Diversity Council, which includes staff members from a variety of demographic backgrounds and represents all divisions and levels, I have come to realize that pursuing traditional methods of developing future managers will not itself increase diversity significantly at the highest levels.

I am convinced that in order to ensure a better future, changes must begin with those at the top of the corporation. We've created a task force whose charge is to develop specific recommendations for ways in which Quaker can identify, nurture, retain, and advance women and minority executives. To make this work, we will have to set measurable goals, carefully and continuously monitor our progress, reward those managers who successfully carry out this mandate, and penalize those who don't. As a consumer products company, our guiding marketing principle is to stay close to our customers. To be successful, our internal policies and the makeup of our top management must reflect this principle as well. In the best interests of their company's future, Vision Software's senior executives should follow suit.

Jay M. Jackman, M.D., is a private-practice psychiatrist in Stanford, California, and a consultant for organizational change, with a particular interest in the "glass ceiling." Myra H. Strober is a labor economist at the School of Education at Stanford University and a consultant on issues of employment of women and minorities.

As any good mountaineer will tell you, a successful ascent requires a good deal of preparation: choosing fellow climbers, ensuring team conditioning, assembling first-rate equipment, and hiring experienced guides. Raising issues of sexism with the CEO of a corporation requires similar preparation. Liz definitely should discuss the issues of gender stonewalling at Vision Software with Clark but not alone, not yet, and not by memo.

Liz should not underestimate the difficulty of the mountain she has set out to climb. The undermining of women in the workplace is both common and difficult to change. It stems from a complicated interaction of men's beliefs and behaviors, women's beliefs and behaviors, the structures and procedures set up by companies, and the ways in which we organize and run our families. That the behaviors Liz cites have gone on for at least ten years without the CEO's

If the Dinosaur Won't Change. . .

OVER THE LAST TWENTY YEARS, the percentage of women business owners has grown from 5% to over 30% and is still rising. By the end of 1992, more people will work in companies owned by women than will work in the *Fortune* 500. Liz helps us see why. If the dinosaur won't change, it will become extinct.

After years of banging heads against glass ceilings, huge numbers of women are realizing that learning how to dress, getting the right degrees, and struggling to fit in are essentially, fruitless exercises. Of a certain age and self-awareness, women who are weary of trying to adapt to environments in which they are not welcome are leaving to create companies that fit them. The woman who feels strongly enough to write a memo is in the process of breaking with an unfriendly culture. Whether she sends it or not is unimportant—the process of alienation has begun. And if she chooses not to spend another calorie of energy teaching lessons that companies have had over two decades to learn—and are in their own best interests—that is her prerogative.

In fact, the Harvard Business School itself has documented the case of a woman whose ideas were rejected as "not workable" in a corporation. She eventually left that company and went on to start not one, but two highly successful companies ("Ruth M. Owades," HBS 9-383-051, revised Feb. 1985). Tired of sending memos and sounding alarms, women are taking charge of their lives. What the leadership of the company does to address its workforce challenges will spell the survival or extinction of the company, regardless of whether Liz's memo is ever sent.

Joline Godfrey *is the founder and director of An Income of Her Own, a company that specializes in entrepreneurial education for teenage women, and author of* Our Wildest Dreams: Women Making Money, Having Fun, Doing Good *(Harper Business, New York).*

notice (hardly an uncommon situation) underscores the difficulty of change. At the moment, the CEO is part of the problem; Liz's task is to make him part of the solution—no mean feat.

Liz needs to assemble allies: other women in the company, perhaps even some who have left, possibly certain members of the board, or men in the company. Singlehandedly attempting to change Clark's views is as foolhardy as attempting a solo alpine ascent. Also, Liz needs to strengthen the case to be presented to Clark. She needs more than the "anecdotes" she cites in her memo and must give Clark concrete reasons why women are leaving the company, not just speculation.

Liz also must talk with experts. There are many academics and consultants who help women and companies understand the dynamics behind sexist practices and work with them toward change. Successfully approaching a CEO about alleviating sexism—a process that ultimately will require major changes in corporate culture and structure—needs expert guidance.

Finally, we would urge Liz, with one or two people from the group she assembles, to talk to Clark in person rather than sending a memo. At the moment, she has no idea where he stands on the subject of sexism. In a meeting, she can observe when he gets defensive, test his willingness to cooperate, and suggest incremental changes that he is likely to back. Women with ten years of experience in a corporation are precious assets; as they move to improve the system for women in general, they should not sacrifice themselves.

Gloria Steinem is a founder and consulting editor of Ms. *magazine. She also travels widely as a feminist speaker and organizer. She is the author of* Revolution from Within *(Little, Brown).*

Unless Liz is in imminent danger of hunger or homelessness, I would advise her to send the memo. If she doesn't, she is not only acting against her own and other women's long-term interest but also failing to give her company her best advice.

With that in mind, I would also change the memo's tone. Right now, it has a tone of apology and includes no reference at all to the company's goals. Liz should make a case for Vision Software to choose a self-interested path toward inclusiveness for the long-term benefit of the company's employees—and its bottom line. I would advise her to write the memo with the same enthusiasm she would express if she were telling her boss about a new technology that could put Vision ahead of its competitors. Because that is exactly what she's doing: discovering a new technology. Just because it's a "soft" technology of human resources rather than one relating to inanimate objects doesn't mean her discoveries are less important. Indeed, they may be further-reaching and more important. Liz can underscore this by using such "hard" facts as company and

Overcoming the Culture of Exclusion

LIZ AMES'S DILEMMA RAISES a larger issue that permeates corporate life: How is it that we have created institutions in which people are afraid to express the truth as they see it? *Bhopal, Three Mile Island, and the Ford Pinto all were preceded by memos unsent or unread.*

Vision Software is losing out because it operates in a culture of exclusion. The company has suffered and will continue to suffer, both internally and in the marketplace, because it refuses to look clearly at itself. If it cannot intelligently reveal its own inner workings in a way that is collaborative and supportive of its members, then it defies its own mission to produce educational software. The company's mission, and Liz's challenge, is to absorb information from the environment and incorporate that information into an evolving system, whether it be a human being or a corporation—that is what learning is all about.

If we are to re-create our corporate organizations so that they become more socially and environmentally responsible, business will have to learn from nature. All living systems depend on constant feedback loops that recalibrate the organism's relationship to life around it. Vision's corporate culture appears to accept only feedback loops that reinforce maladaptive behavior such as sexist or exclusionary practices.

For that reason Liz has to send her memo. Her career, after all, does depend on it. Maybe not her career within the context of Vision Software—particularly if it is read in an unsympathetic light—but her life goal. Liz has to remember that she set out not only to bring home a paycheck but also to express her own values and qualities in the commercial arena.

If she doesn't file the memo, Liz will be left with the new dilemma of subordinating her own wisdom and sense of self to a system that is not fully functional. She will have an aborted sense of her own value, an acute loss in a world that is crying out for more value to be added to it. If business is about adding value, then what better place to find it than within ourselves.

Paul Hawken *is the author of* The Ecology of Commerce *(HarperCollins, September 1993). He is the founder of Smith & Hawken, a catalog company known for its environmental initiatives, but is no longer affiliated with the company.*

---

industrywide statistics on the cost of losing a trained executive. The goal here is to help the boss see his female employees' problems as his own and thus their solution as his victory. Empathy is the most revolutionary emotion.

What's interesting about this case study, however, is that Liz's male colleague never raises the question of whether he should cosign the memo. Or whether he should offer to support it with one of his own. Or whether he might join her in asking one or more supportive colleagues—male or female—to become part of this process.

These unaddressed options are symbolic of the ways in which sexism is regarded as the problem of women—just as racism is regarded as the problem of people of color—when in fact, those problems limit everyone. Until the more powerful own the responsibility for prejudice, it will continue to cripple us all.

Originally published in March–April 1993. Reprint 93209

Why Diversity Programs Fail

by Frank Dobbin and Alexandra Kalev

BUSINESSES STARTED CARING A LOT more about diversity after a series of high-profile lawsuits rocked the financial industry. In the late 1990s and early 2000s, Morgan Stanley shelled out $54 million—and Smith Barney and Merrill Lynch more than $100 million each—to settle sex discrimination claims. In 2007, Morgan was back at the table, facing a new class action, which cost the company $46 million. In 2013, Bank of America Merrill Lynch settled a race discrimination suit for $160 million. Cases like these brought Merrill's total 15-year payout to nearly *half a billion* dollars.

It's no wonder that Wall Street firms now require new hires to sign arbitration contracts agreeing not to join class actions. They have also expanded training and other diversity programs. But on balance, equality isn't improving in financial services or elsewhere. Although the proportion of managers at U.S. commercial banks who were Hispanic rose from 4.7% in 2003 to 5.7% in 2014, white women's representation dropped from 39% to 35%, and black men's from 2.5% to 2.3%. The numbers were even worse in investment banks (though that industry is shrinking, which complicates the analysis). Among all U.S. companies with 100 or more employees, the proportion of black men in management increased just slightly—from 3% to 3.3%—from 1985 to 2014. White women saw bigger gains from 1985 to 2000—rising from 22% to 29% of managers—but their numbers haven't budged since then. Even in Silicon Valley, where many leaders tout the need to increase diversity for both business and social justice reasons, bread-and-butter tech jobs remain dominated by white men.

It shouldn't be surprising that most diversity programs aren't increasing diversity. Despite a few new bells and whistles, courtesy of big data, companies are basically doubling down on the same approaches they've used since the 1960s—which often make things worse, not better. Firms have long relied on diversity training to reduce bias on the job, hiring tests and performance ratings to limit it in recruitment and promotions, and grievance systems to give employees a way to challenge managers. Those tools are designed to preempt lawsuits by policing managers' thoughts and actions. Yet laboratory studies show that this kind of force-feeding can activate bias rather than stamp it out. As social scientists have found, people often rebel against rules to assert their autonomy. Try to coerce me to do X, Y, or Z, and I'll do the opposite just to prove that I'm my own person.

In analyzing three decades' worth of data from more than 800 U.S. firms and interviewing hundreds of line managers and executives at length, we've seen that companies get better results when they ease up on the control tactics. It's more effective to engage managers in solving the problem, increase their on-the-job contact with female and minority workers, and promote social accountability—the desire to look fair-minded. That's why interventions such as targeted college recruitment, mentoring programs, self-managed teams, and task forces have boosted diversity in businesses. Some of the most effective solutions aren't even designed with diversity in mind.

Here, we dig into the data, the interviews, and company examples to shed light on what doesn't work and what does.

Why You Can't Just Outlaw Bias

Executives favor a classic command-and-control approach to diversity because it boils expected behaviors down to dos and don'ts that are easy to understand and defend. Yet this approach also flies in the

Idea in Brief

The Problem

To reduce bias and increase diversity, organizations are relying on the same programs they've been using since the 1960s. Some of these efforts make matters worse, not better.

The Reason

Most diversity programs focus on controlling managers' behavior, and as studies show, that approach tends to activate bias rather than quash it. People rebel against rules that threaten their autonomy.

The Solution

Instead of trying to police managers' decisions, the most effective programs engage people in working for diversity, increase their contact with women and minorities, and tap into their desire to look good to others.

face of nearly everything we know about how to motivate people to make changes. Decades of social science research point to a simple truth: You won't get managers on board by blaming and shaming them with rules and reeducation. Let's look at how the most common top-down efforts typically go wrong.

Diversity training

Do people who undergo training usually shed their biases? Researchers have been examining that question since before World War II, in nearly a thousand studies. It turns out that while people are easily taught to respond correctly to a questionnaire about bias, they soon forget the right answers. The positive effects of diversity training rarely last beyond a day or two, and a number of studies suggest that it can activate bias or spark a backlash. Nonetheless, nearly half of midsize companies use it, as do nearly all the *Fortune* 500.

Many firms see adverse effects. One reason is that three-quarters use negative messages in their training. By headlining the legal case for diversity and trotting out stories of huge settlements, they issue an implied threat: "Discriminate, and the company will pay the price." We understand the temptation—that's how we got your attention in the first paragraph—but threats, or "negative incentives," don't win converts.

Another reason is that about three-quarters of firms with training still follow the dated advice of the late diversity guru R. Roosevelt Thomas Jr. "If diversity management is strategic to the organization," he used to say, diversity training must be mandatory, and management has to make it clear that "if you can't deal with that, then we have to ask you to leave." But five years after instituting required training for managers, companies saw no improvement in the proportion of white women, black men, and Hispanics in management, and the share of black women actually decreased by 9%, on average, while the ranks of Asian-American men and women shrank by 4% to 5%. Trainers tell us that people often respond to compulsory courses with anger and resistance—and many participants actually report more animosity toward other groups afterward.

But voluntary training evokes the opposite response ("I chose to show up, so I must be pro-diversity"), leading to better results: increases of 9% to 13% in black men, Hispanic men, and Asian-American men and women in management five years out (with no decline in white or black women). Research from the University of Toronto reinforces our findings: In one study white subjects read a brochure critiquing prejudice toward blacks. When people felt pressure to agree with it, the reading strengthened their bias against blacks. When they felt the choice was theirs, the reading reduced bias.

Companies too often signal that training is remedial. The diversity manager at a national beverage company told us that the top brass uses it to deal with problem groups. "If there are a number of complaints. . . or, God forbid, some type of harassment case. . . leaders say, 'Everyone in the business unit will go through it again.'" Most companies with training have special programs for managers. To be sure, they're a high-risk group because they make the hiring, promotion, and pay decisions. But singling them out implies that they're the worst culprits. Managers tend to resent that implication and resist the message.

Hiring tests

Some 40% of companies now try to fight bias with mandatory hiring tests assessing the skills of candidates for frontline jobs. But managers don't like being told that they can't hire whomever they please, and our research suggests that they often use the tests selectively. Back in the 1950s, following the postwar migration of blacks northward, Swift & Company, Chicago meatpackers, instituted tests for supervisor and quality-checking jobs. One study found managers telling blacks that they had failed the test and then promoting whites who hadn't been tested. A black machine operator reported: "I had four years at Englewood High School. I took an exam for a checker's job. The foreman told me I failed" and gave the job to a white man who "didn't take the exam."

This kind of thing still happens. When we interviewed the new HR director at a West Coast food company, he said he found that white managers were making only strangers—most of them minorities— take supervisor tests and hiring white friends without testing them. "If you are going to test one person for this particular job title," he told us, "you need to test everybody."

But even managers who test everyone applying for a position may ignore the results. Investment banks and consulting firms build tests into their job interviews, asking people to solve math and scenario-based problems on the spot. While studying this practice, Kellogg professor Lauren Rivera played a fly on the wall during hiring meetings at one firm. She found that the team paid little attention when white men blew the math test but close attention when women and blacks did. Because decision makers (deliberately or not) cherry-picked results, the testing amplified bias rather than quashed it.

Companies that institute written job tests for managers—about 10% have them today—see decreases of 4% to 10% in the share of managerial jobs held by white women, African-American men and women, Hispanic men and women, and Asian-American women over the next five years. There are significant declines among white and Asian-American women—groups with high levels of education, which typically score well on standard managerial tests. So group differences in test-taking skills don't explain the pattern.

Performance ratings
More than 90% of midsize and large companies use annual performance ratings to ensure that managers make fair pay and promotion

decisions. Identifying and rewarding the best workers isn't the only goal—the ratings also provide a litigation shield. Companies sued for discrimination often claim that their performance rating systems prevent biased treatment.

But studies show that raters tend to lowball women and minorities in performance reviews. And some managers give everyone high marks to avoid hassles with employees or to keep their options open when handing out promotions. However managers work around performance systems, the bottom line is that ratings don't boost diversity. When companies introduce them, there's no effect on minority managers over the next five years, and the share of white women in management drops by 4%, on average.

Grievance procedures

This last tactic is meant to identify and rehabilitate biased managers. About half of midsize and large firms have systems through which employees can challenge pay, promotion, and termination decisions. But many managers—rather than change their own behavior or address discrimination by others—try to get even with or belittle employees who complain. Among the nearly 90,000 discrimination complaints made to the Equal Employment Opportunity Commission in 2015, 45% included a charge of retaliation—which suggests that the original report was met with ridicule, demotion, or worse.

Once people see that a grievance system isn't warding off bad behavior in their organization, they may become less likely to speak up. Indeed, employee surveys show that most people don't report discrimination. This leads to another unintended consequence: Managers who receive few complaints conclude that their firms don't have a problem. We see this a lot in our interviews. When we talked with the vice president of HR at an electronics firm, she mentioned the widely publicized "difficulties other corporations are having" and added, "We have not had any of those problems . . . we have gone almost four years without any kind of discrimination complaint!" What's more, lab studies show that protective measures like grievance systems lead people to drop their guard and let bias affect their decisions, because they think company policies will guarantee fairness.

Things don't get better when firms put in formal grievance systems; they get worse. Our quantitative analyses show that the managerial ranks of white women and all minority groups except Hispanic men decline—by 3% to 11%—in the five years after companies adopt them.

Still, most employers feel they need some sort of system to intercept complaints, if only because judges like them. One strategy that is gaining ground is the "flexible" complaint system, which offers not only a formal hearing process but also informal mediation. Since an informal resolution doesn't involve hauling the manager before a disciplinary body, it may reduce retaliation. As we'll show, making managers feel accountable without subjecting them to public rebuke tends to help.

Tools for Getting Managers on Board

If these popular solutions backfire, then what can employers do instead to promote diversity?

A number of companies have gotten consistently positive results with tactics that don't focus on control. They apply three basic principles: engage managers in solving the problem, expose them to people from different groups, and encourage social accountability for change.

Engagement

When someone's beliefs and behavior are out of sync, that person experiences what psychologists call "cognitive dissonance." Experiments show that people have a strong tendency to "correct" dissonance by changing either the beliefs or the behavior. So, if you prompt them to act in ways that support a particular view, their opinions shift toward that view. Ask them to write an essay defending the death penalty, and even the penalty's staunch opponents will come to see some merits. When managers actively help boost diversity in their companies, something similar happens: They begin to think of themselves as diversity champions.

Take *college recruitment programs* targeting women and minorities. Our interviews suggest that managers willingly participate when invited. That's partly because the message is positive: "Help us find a greater variety of promising employees!" And involvement is voluntary: Executives sometimes single out managers they think would be good recruiters, but they don't drag anyone along at gunpoint.

Managers who make college visits say they take their charge seriously. They are determined to come back with strong candidates from underrepresented groups—female engineers, for instance, or African-American management trainees. Cognitive dissonance soon kicks in—and managers who were wishy-washy about diversity become converts.

The effects are striking. Five years after a company implements a college recruitment program targeting female employees, the share of white women, black women, Hispanic women, and Asian-American women in its management rises by about 10%, on average. A program focused on minority recruitment increases the proportion of black male managers by 8% and black female managers by 9%.

Mentoring is another way to engage managers and chip away at their biases. In teaching their protégés the ropes and sponsoring them for key training and assignments, mentors help give their charges the breaks they need to develop and advance. The mentors then come to believe that their protégés merit these opportunities— whether they're white men, women, or minorities. That is cognitive dissonance—"Anyone I sponsor must be deserving"—at work again.

While white men tend to find mentors on their own, women and minorities more often need help from formal programs. One reason, as Georgetown's business school dean David Thomas discovered in his research on mentoring, is that white male executives don't feel comfortable reaching out informally to young women and minority men. Yet they are eager to mentor assigned protégés, and women and minorities are often first to sign up for mentors.

Mentoring programs make companies' managerial echelons significantly more diverse: On average they boost the representation of black, Hispanic, and Asian-American women, and Hispanic and Asian-American men, by 9% to 24%. In industries where plenty of college-educated nonmanagers are eligible to move up, like chemicals and electronics, mentoring programs also increase the ranks of white women and black men by 10% or more.

Only about 15% of firms have special college recruitment programs for women and minorities, and only 10% have mentoring programs. Once organizations try them out, though, the upside becomes clear. Consider how these programs helped Coca-Cola in the wake of a race discrimination suit settled in 2000 for a record $193 million. With guidance from a court-appointed external task force, executives in the North America group got involved in recruitment and mentoring initiatives for professionals and middle managers, working specifically toward measurable goals for minorities. Even top leaders helped to recruit and mentor, and talent-sourcing partners were required to broaden their recruitment efforts. After five years, according to former CEO and chairman Neville Isdell, 80% of all mentees had climbed at least one rung in management. Both individual and group mentoring were open to all races but attracted large numbers of African-Americans (who accounted for 36% of protégés). These changes brought important gains. From 2000 to 2006, African-Americans' representation among salaried employees grew from 19.7% to 23%, and Hispanics' from 5.5% to 6.4%. And while African-Americans and Hispanics respectively made up 12% and 4.9% of professionals and middle managers in 2002, just four years later those figures had risen to 15.5% and 5.9%.

This began a virtuous cycle. Today, Coke looks like a different company. This February, *Atlanta Tribune* magazine profiled 17 African-American women in VP roles and above at Coke, including CFO Kathy Waller.

Contact

Evidence that contact between groups can lessen bias first came to light in an unplanned experiment on the European front during World War II. The U.S. army was still segregated, and only whites served in combat roles. High casualties left General Dwight

Eisenhower understaffed, and he asked for black volunteers for combat duty. When Harvard sociologist Samuel Stouffer, on leave at the War Department, surveyed troops on their racial attitudes, he found that whites whose companies had been joined by black platoons showed dramatically lower racial animus and greater willingness to work alongside blacks than those whose companies remained segregated. Stouffer concluded that whites fighting alongside blacks came to see them as soldiers like themselves first and foremost. The key, for Stouffer, was that whites and blacks had to be working toward a common goal *as equals*—hundreds of years of close contact during and after slavery hadn't dampened bias.

Business practices that generate this kind of contact across groups yield similar results. Take *self-managed teams,* which allow people in different roles and functions to work together on projects as equals. Such teams increase contact among diverse types of people, because specialties within firms are still largely divided along racial, ethnic, and gender lines. For example, women are more likely than men to work in sales, whereas white men are more likely to be in tech jobs and management, and black and Hispanic men are more likely to be in production.

As in Stouffer's combat study, working side-by-side breaks down stereotypes, which leads to more equitable hiring and promotion. At firms that create self-managed work teams, the share of white women, black men and women, and Asian-American women in management rises by 3% to 6% over five years.

Rotating management trainees through departments is another way to increase contact. Typically, this kind of *cross-training* allows people to try their hand at various jobs and deepen their understanding of the whole organization. But it also has a positive impact on diversity, because it exposes both department heads and trainees to a wider variety of people. The result, we've seen, is a bump of 3% to 7% in white women, black men and women, and Asian-American men and women in management.

About a third of U.S. firms have self-managed teams for core operations, and nearly four-fifths use cross-training, so these tools are already available in many organizations. Though college recruitment

The Downside of the Diversity Label

WHY CAN MENTORING, self-managed teams, and cross-training increase diversity without the backlash prompted by mandatory training? One reason may be that these programs aren't usually branded as diversity efforts. Diversity language in company policy can stress white men out, as researchers at UC Santa Barbara and the University of Washington found when they put young white men through a simulated job interview—half of them for a company that touted its commitment to diversity, and half for a company that did not. In the explicitly pro-diversity company, subjects expected discrimination against whites, showed cardiovascular distress, and did markedly worse in the taped interview.

and mentoring have a bigger impact on diversity—perhaps because they activate engagement in the diversity mission *and* create intergroup contact—every bit helps. Self-managed teams and cross-training have had more positive effects than mandatory diversity training, performance evaluations, job testing, or grievance procedures, which are supposed to promote diversity.

Social accountability

The third tactic, encouraging social accountability, plays on our need to look good in the eyes of those around us. It is nicely illustrated by an experiment conducted in Israel. Teachers in training graded identical compositions attributed to Jewish students with Ashkenazic names (European heritage) or with Sephardic names (African or Asian heritage). Sephardic students typically come from poorer families and do worse in school. On average, the teacher trainees gave the Ashkenazic essays Bs and the Sephardic essays Ds. The difference evaporated, however, when trainees were told that they would discuss their grades with peers. The idea that they might have to explain their decisions led them to judge the work by its quality.

In the workplace you'll see a similar effect. Consider this field study conducted by Emilio Castilla of MIT's Sloan School of Management: A firm found it consistently gave African-Americans smaller raises than whites, even when they had identical job titles and performance ratings. So Castilla suggested transparency to activate social accountability. The firm posted each unit's average performance rating and pay raise by race and gender. Once managers realized that employees, peers, and superiors would know which parts of the company favored whites, the gap in raises all but disappeared.

Corporate *diversity task forces* help promote social accountability. CEOs usually assemble these teams, inviting department heads to volunteer and including members of underrepresented groups. Every quarter or two, task forces look at diversity numbers for the whole company, for business units, and for departments to figure out what needs attention.

After investigating where the problems are—recruitment, career bottlenecks, and so on—task force members come up with solutions, which they then take back to their departments. They notice if their colleagues aren't volunteering to mentor or showing up at recruitment events. Accountability theory suggests that having a task force member in a department will cause managers in it to ask themselves, "Will this look right?" when making hiring and promotion decisions.

Deloitte has seen how powerful social accountability can be. In 1992, Mike Cook, who was then the CEO, decided to try to stanch the hemorrhaging of female associates. Half the company's hires were women, but nearly all of them left before they were anywhere near making partner. As Douglas McCracken, CEO of Deloitte's consulting unit at the time, later recounted in HBR, Cook assembled a high-profile task force that "didn't immediately launch a slew of new organizational policies aimed at outlawing bad behavior" but, rather, relied on transparency to get results.

The task force got each office to monitor the career progress of its women and set its own goals to address local problems. When it became clear that the CEO and other managing partners were closely watching, McCracken wrote, "women started getting their share of premier client assignments and informal mentoring." And unit heads all over the country began getting questions from partners and associates about why things weren't changing faster. An external advisory council issued annual progress reports, and individual managers chose change metrics to add to their own performance ratings. In eight years turnover among women dropped to the same level as turnover among men, and the proportion of female partners increased from 5% to 14%—the highest percentage among the big accounting firms. By 2015, 21% of Deloitte's global partners were women, and in March of that year, Deloitte LLP appointed Cathy Engelbert as its CEO—making her the first woman to head a major accountancy.

Task forces are the trifecta of diversity programs. In addition to promoting accountability, they engage members who might have previously been cool to diversity projects and increase contact among the women, minorities, and white men who participate. They pay off, too: On average, companies that put in diversity task forces see 9% to 30% increases in the representation of white women and of each minority group in management over the next five years.

Diversity managers, too, boost inclusion by creating social accountability. To see why, let's go back to the finding of the teacher-in-training experiment, which is supported by many studies: When people know they *might* have to explain their decisions, they are less likely to act on bias. So simply having a diversity manager who could ask them questions prompts managers to step back and consider everyone who is qualified instead of hiring or promoting the first people who come to mind. Companies that appoint diversity managers see 7% to 18% increases in all underrepresented groups—except Hispanic men—in management in the following five years. Those are the gains after accounting for both effective and ineffective programs they put in place.

Only 20% of medium and large employers have task forces, and just 10% have diversity managers, despite the benefits of both. Diversity managers cost money, but task forces use existing workers, so they're a lot cheaper than some of the things that fail, such as mandatory training.

Leading companies like Bank of America Merrill Lynch, Facebook, and Google have placed big bets on accountability in the past couple of years. Expanding on Deloitte's early example, they're now

Which Diversity Efforts Actually Succeed?

IN 829 MIDSIZE AND LARGE U.S. FIRMS, we analyzed how various diversity initiatives affected the proportion of women and minorities in management. Here you can see which ones helped different groups gain ground—and which

Poor Returns on the Usual Programs

The three most popular interventions made firms less diverse, not more, because managers resisted strong-arming.

% Change over five years

MANDATORY DIVERSITY TRAINING for managers led to significant decreases for Asian-Americans and black women.

TESTING job applicants hurt women and minorities—but not because they perform poorly. Hiring managers don't always test everyone (white men often get a pass) and don't interpret results consistently.

Programs That Get Results

Companies do a better job of increasing diversity when they forgo the control tactics and frame their efforts more positively. The most effective programs spark engagement, increase contact among different groups, or draw on people's strong desire to look good to others.

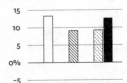

VOLUNTARY TRAINING doesn't get managers' defenses up the way mandatory training does—and results in increases for several groups.

SELF-MANAGED TEAMS aren't designed to improve diversity, but they help by increasing contact between groups, which are often concentrated in certain functions.

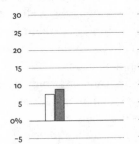

COLLEGE RECRUITMENT TARGETING MINORITIES often focuses on historically black schools, which lifts the numbers of African-American men and women.

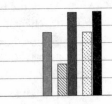

MENTORING has an especially positive impact. Managers who sponsor women and minorities come to believe, through their increased contact, that their protégés deserve the training and opportunities they've received.

set them back, despite good intentions. (No bar means we can't say with statistical certainty if the program had any effect.)

GRIEVANCE SYSTEMS
likewise reduced diversity pretty much across the board. Though they're meant to reform biased managers, they often lead to retaliation.

☑ White men
☐ White women

☐ Black men
▨ Black women

◩ Hispanic men
▧ Hispanic women

⊡ Asian men
■ Asian women

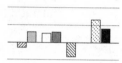

CROSS-TRAINING also increases managers' exposure to people from different groups. Gains for some groups appear to come at a cost to Hispanic men.

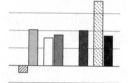

COLLEGE RECRUITMENT TARGETING WOMEN turns recruiting managers into diversity champions, so it also helps boost the numbers for black and Asian-American men.

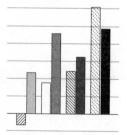

DIVERSITY TASK FORCES
promote social accountability because members bring solutions back to their departments—and notice whether their colleagues adopt them.

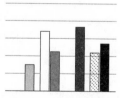

DIVERSITY MANAGERS
sometimes put ineffective programs in place but have a positive impact overall— in part because managers know someone might ask them about their hiring and promotion decisions.

Note: In our analysis, we've isolated the effects of diversity programs from everything else going on in the companies and in the economy.

posting complete diversity numbers for all to see. We should know in a few years if that moves the needle for them.

Strategies for controlling bias—which drive most diversity efforts—have failed spectacularly since they were introduced to promote equal opportunity. Black men have barely gained ground in corporate management since 1985. White women haven't progressed since 2000. It isn't that there aren't enough educated women and minorities out there—both groups have made huge educational gains over the past two generations. The problem is that we can't motivate people by forcing them to get with the program and punishing them if they don't.

The numbers sum it up. Your organization will become less diverse, not more, if you require managers to go to diversity training, try to regulate their hiring and promotion decisions, and put in a legalistic grievance system.

The very good news is that we know what does work—we just need to do more of it.

Originally published in July–August 2016. Reprint R1607C

Now What?

by Joan C. Williams and Suzanne Lebsock

FAREWELL TO THE WORLD where men can treat the workplace like a frat house or a pornography shoot. Since Hollywood producer Harvey Weinstein was accused of sexual misconduct in early October, similar allegations have been made about nearly 100 other powerful people. They all are names you probably recognize, in fields including media, technology, hospitality, politics, and entertainment. It's a watershed moment for workplace equality and safety; 87% of Americans now favor zero tolerance of sexual harassment.

Not only is this better for women, but it's better for most men. A workplace culture in which sexual harassment is rampant is often one that also shames men who refuse to participate. These men-who-don't-fit, like the mistreated women, face choices about whether and how to intervene without endangering their careers.

Still, it's unnerving for many men to see the numbers of those toppled by accusations grow ever higher. The recent summary dismissals of high-powered executives and celebrities have triggered worries that any man might be accused and ruined. Half of men (49%) say the recent furor has made them think again about their own behavior around women. Men wonder whether yesterday's sophomoric idiocy is today's career wrecker.

This is not a fight between men and women, however. One of the journalists to break the Weinstein story was Ronan Farrow, son of Mia Farrow and Woody Allen. Yes, that Woody Allen—the one who married his longtime girlfriend's daughter and is alleged to have sexually abused another daughter. "Sexual assault was an issue that had touched my family," said Farrow, who noted that this experience was instrumental in driving his reporting.

To repeat: This is not a fight between men and women. It's a fight over whether a small subgroup of predatory men should be allowed to interfere with people's ability to show up and do what they signed up for: work.

Several changes in the past decade have brought us to this startling moment. Some were technological: The internet enables women to go public with accusations, bypassing the gatekeepers who traditionally buried their stories. Other changes were cultural: A centuries-old stereotype—the Vengeful Lying Slut—was drained of its power by feminists who coined the term "slut shaming" and reverse-shamed those who did it. Just as important, women have made enough inroads into positions of power in the press, corporations, Congress, and Hollywood that they no longer have to play along with the boys' club; instead they can, say, lead the charge to force Al Franken's resignation or break the story on Harvey Weinstein.

The result of all these changes is what social scientists call a norms cascade: a series of long-term trends that produce a sudden shift in social mores. There's no going back. The work environment now is much different from what it was a year ago. To put things plainly, if you sexually harass or assault a colleague, employee, boss, or business contact today, your job will be at risk.

How the #MeToo Movement Changes Work

As commonplace as these dismissals have come to seem, we know that we are only beginning to scratch the surface of the harassment culture. In "You Can't Change What You Can't See: Interrupting Racial & Gender Bias in the Legal Profession," a forthcoming study of lawyers conducted by the Center for WorkLife Law (which Joan directs) for the American Bar Association, researchers found sexual harassment to be pervasive. Eighty-two percent of women and 74% of men reported hearing sexist comments at work. Twenty-eight

Idea in Brief

When Hollywood producer Harvey Weinstein was accused of sexual harassment, the dam broke. Allegations of sexual misconduct were raised against many powerful people, and millions of women shared their own stories of harassment. It's a watershed moment for equality, say Williams, a legal scholar, and Lebsock, a feminist historian. Now 87% of Americans favor zero tolerance of harassment. Half of men are rethinking their own behavior. Over 75% of people are more likely to report sexist treatment at work. Everything has changed, for a simple reason: Women are being believed. Such was not the case in 1991, when Anita Hill claimed harassment by Supreme Court justice nominee Clarence Thomas. Back then women who came forward were often discredited as "vengeful, lying sluts." But that stereotype has been drained of power by feminists who coined the term "slut-shaming" and reverse-shamed those who did it. As the #MeToo and Time's Up movements demonstrate, women

will no longer be silenced. Translating outrage into action requires new norms of workplace conduct, which the authors outline. Firms are moving away from quiet settlements with victims and toward firing abusers. But employers still must follow due process and evaluate the credibility of reports. They need clear policies and fair procedures for handling harassment. No one's asking men to stop being men. But the reasonable assumption is that work relationships should be about work. You must not take one in a romantic direction if it's unwelcome, and the only way to safely tell what someone else wants is to ask. At the same time men shouldn't avoid women at work. That's unnecessary, unfair, and illegal: It deprives women of opportunities simply because of their gender. Women, if colleagues make you uncomfortable, tell them. If you're harassed, report it. The authors aren't sure they'd have said that before #MeToo, but they do now, and it signals that the world has changed.

percent of women and 8% of men reported unwanted sexual or romantic attention or touching at work. Seven percent of women and less than 1% of men reported being bribed or threatened with workplace consequences if they did not engage in sexual behavior. Fourteen percent of women and 5% of men said that they had lost work opportunities because of sexual harassment, which was also associated with delays in promotions, reduced access to high-profile assignments and sponsorship, bias against parents, and higher intent to leave. The three most acute types of harassment (excluding sexist remarks) were associated with reductions in income, demotions, loss of clients and office space, and removal from important committees.

These patterns hold true beyond the legal profession. According to a recent study by researchers at Oklahoma State University, the University of Minnesota, and the University of Maine, women who were sexually harassed were 6.5 times as likely to change jobs as women who weren't. "I quit, and I didn't have a job. That's it. I'm outta here. I'll eat rice and live in the dark if I have to," remarked one woman in the study.

Low-wage women, who often live paycheck to paycheck, and women who are working in the U.S. illegally are the most vulnerable. A survey of nearly 500 Chicago hotel housekeepers revealed that 49% had encountered a guest who had exposed himself. Janitors who work the graveyard shift and farmworkers have had trouble defending themselves against predatory supervisors. And restaurant workers experience it from three directions. A 2014 report aptly titled "The Glass Floor," which shares the findings of a survey of 688 restaurant workers from 39 states, reveals that nearly 80% of the female workers had been harassed by colleagues. Nearly 80% had been harassed by customers, and 67% had been harassed by managers—52% of them on a weekly basis. Workers found customer harassment especially vexing because they were loath to lose crucial income from tips. Small wonder that almost 37% of sexual harassment complaints filed by women with the Equal Employment Opportunity Commission in 2011 came from the restaurant industry.

The stories finally becoming public further highlight how sexual harassment subverts women's careers: Ashley Judd and Mira Sorvino found acting jobs harder to get after they rebuffed the voracious Weinstein. After Gretchen Carlson complained of a hostile work environment, she was assigned fewer hard-hitting interviews on *Fox & Friends* and, according to her legal complaint, was cut from her weekly appearances on the highly rated "Culture

Warrior" segment of *The O'Reilly Factor*. Because word got out that Ninth Circuit judge Alex Kozinski sexually harassed clerks, many women did not apply for a clerkship at that court, which positions young lawyers to get clerkships at the U.S. Supreme Court—the biggest plum in the legal basket. When the ambitious congressional staffer Lauren Greene complained of sexual harassment by her boss, Representative Blake Farenthold, her career in politics evaporated. Today she works as a part-time assistant to a home builder.

A point often overlooked is that some sexual harassment victims are men. Men filed nearly 17% of sexual harassment complaints with the EEOC in 2016. Some men are harassed by women, but many are harassed by other men, some straight, some gay. A roustabout on an oil platform was harassed by coworkers on his eight-man crew, the U.S. Supreme Court found in 1998; the coworkers were offended by what they perceived as his insufficient machismo. Recently the Metropolitan Opera suspended longtime conductor James Levine after several men accused him of masturbation-heavy abuse that took place from the late 1960s to the 1980s, when his victims were 16 to 20 years old.

Such behavior is no longer seen as a "tsking" matter. Historically, it has been hard to win a sexual harassment suit, but rapidly shifting public perceptions may change that. Seventy-eight percent of women say they are more likely to speak out now if they are treated unfairly because of their gender. About the same percentage of men (77%) say they are now more likely to speak out if they see a woman being treated unfairly. It's a new day for a simple reason: Women are being believed.

Everything Is Changing

The strongest indicator that we're experiencing a norms cascade came when Senate Majority Leader Mitch McConnell stood up for the women—four of them at the time—who had come forward with revelations about senatorial candidate Roy Moore.

"I believe the women," McConnell said.

The statement stands in stark contrast to Anita Hill's treatment in 1991, when she testified before the Senate Judiciary Committee that Clarence Thomas, then a nominee to the Supreme Court, had sexually harassed her. Senators subjected her to a humiliating inquisition, watched by a rapt national television audience. Another former employee was waiting in the wings to describe how Thomas had sexually harassed her, too. But she was never called to testify. Instead, Hill withstood the all-male committee's bullying alone. After the hearings, opposition to Hill made her life at the University of Oklahoma so difficult that she left her tenured position—an object lesson on the risks facing anyone who dared to raise a charge of sexual harassment.

A recent poll by NPR dramatizes the sudden shift: 66% of Americans think that women who reported sexual harassment were generally ignored five years ago. Only 26% think that women are ignored today. When did we begin believing the women? What changed? And what are the implications for men?

We can trace the disbelief of—or at best, disregard for—women to the old stereotype we mentioned earlier, the one that holds women to be fundamentally irrational, vengeful, deceitful, and rampantly sexual.

An ancient version of this stereotype appears in Genesis, in which Eve commits the first sin and then drags Adam and the rest of humanity down with her for all time. Through the ages in Judeo-Christian tradition, authors expounded upon feminine evil. Among the most vivid prose stylists were two German friars, who in 1486 produced the classic book of witch lore *The Malleus Maleficarum* (or *The Hammer of Witches*). "What else is woman but a foe to friendship, an unescapable punishment, a necessary evil, a natural temptation, a desirable calamity, a domestic danger, a delectable detriment, an evil of nature, painted with fair colours!" they wrote. More to the point for us, perhaps, is their claim that a woman "is a liar by nature."

Although by the 19th century more-positive images of women arose, the stereotype of the Vengeful Lying Slut was too useful to die. It was imposed on entire classes of women, notably African-American women, as scholars have amply documented, and on working-class women pressured into sex by bosses. It was used to ostracize and humiliate high schoolers who found themselves suddenly disparaged as "easy." Whenever men, and sometimes boys, exploited women—or often girls—the stereotype of the Vengeful Lying Slut supplied the words to justify their behavior: She wanted it/asked for it/had it coming.

The stereotype alas persists. It underlies men's fears that they, too, will be brought down by false allegations. Some men have become so frightened that they now refuse to meet (or to eat with) a female colleague alone. When Roy Moore was accused of sexual assault, his campaign said he was the victim of a "witch hunt." That response is a telling and time-honored way of discrediting victims.

The #MeToo and Time's Up movements show that women can no longer be silenced by threats of slut shaming. When a manager at Google told one of the female engineers who worked there, "It's taking all my self-control not to grab your ass right now," she tweeted it out to the world. In the first 24 hours after actress Alyssa Milano suggested that victims of harassment reply "me too" to a tweet in October, 12 million women made #MeToo posts on Facebook. Instead of distancing themselves from those challenging sexual harassment, as might have happened in the past, actors and actresses wore black to the 2018 Golden Globes to signal their solidarity.

Translating outrage into action, however, requires moving beyond hashtags toward new norms of workplace conduct. It's a precarious moment, and a lot could go wrong. Just think what might have happened if the *Washington Post*, with admirable rigor, had not uncovered the truth when a woman approached it with a dramatic but false accusation against Roy Moore. Her purpose? To snooker the *Post* into publishing a bogus story and to thereby cast doubt on all mainstream media reporting the claims against Moore. But so far so good, with early signs that workplaces are indeed changing.

Firing Is the New Settlement

In the past companies often quietly paid to settle sexual harassment complaints against high-powered miscreants and tried to limit the damage through nondisclosure agreements. Incidents at Fox gave rise to at least seven settlements (some against Fox, some against individuals at Fox). Weinstein reportedly paid out eight. Despite getting large payouts, the plaintiffs were the ones who were forced to leave their companies, and many suffered career interruptions.

Quiet settlements are now becoming harder to justify. The unceremonious firings and forced resignations of famous men demonstrate that companies are moving away from that strategy. Settlements will likely continue in some circumstances, such as a first offense involving mild or ambiguous behavior or a situation that is consensual but violates company standards. But long strings of settlements in egregious cases will increasingly be seen as a breach of the directors' duty to the company. Boards of directors have never tolerated financial fraud and violations of the Foreign Corrupt Practices Act, and they are likely to adopt the same standards for harassment—firing without severance pay.

It's important to recognize that most of the firings have occurred at companies with sophisticated legal and HR departments, on the advice of counsel and with the involvement of senior management or the board or both. We should not assume that they are disclosing all the evidence they have. Companies have a strong motive not to release such evidence, lest the former employee use it as ammunition in a defamation or wrongful discharge suit. That's what companies do when they sack someone for cause, and that's what they are doing here.

Some worry that people will be fired too quickly and without due process. One point that's often overlooked: Due process isn't required of private employers, only public ones. What people are trying to insist on, quite properly, are fair procedures that uncover the truth. Companies should follow the same procedures they use when an employee has been accused of any type of serious misconduct. Typically, the employee is placed on leave while an investigation is performed. In most cases, although not all, that's what has been happening with sexual harassment cases.

Credibility assessments are, of course, important. Women are human beings, and sometimes human beings—male and female—

lie. That's why we need to apply the standard methods we always use to assess credibility. Those methods are flawed, but they are all we have; if they will do for every other context, they will do for sexual harassment, too.

As we enter this new era, here's a comforting thought from someone who has spent his life thinking about how to ferret out the truth, the prominent evidence scholar Roger Park (a colleague of Joan's). His observation about sexual harassment is this: "Men have a motive to do it and lie, whereas women don't have a motivation to lie, considering what an ordeal it is." Making even *true* allegations of sexual harassment has historically been a poor career move.

That provides some assurance that reports of harassment are truthful. So do large numbers of people with similar stories. At least 42 women have come forward with allegations against Weinstein, and at least 10 against Ken Friedman, the New York restaurateur. At least a dozen people have made accusations against Kevin Spacey. Those numbers lend credibility to the allegations.

Employers who want to set up processes for handling harassment can begin with the standard sexual harassment policies. The Society for Human Resources has one; others are free online. Organizational training should spell out what's acceptable, which will vary from company to company. Some companies may want to add detail in light of recent events. Surprising as it sounds, some people seem to need a heads-up that porn, kissing, back rubs, and nudity are not appropriate at work.

How can this be? Here's a clue. At a dinner Judge Kozinski held with law clerks, he steered the conversation to the "voluptuous" breasts of a topless woman in a film, according to someone present. When one woman at the dinner reacted negatively, Kozinski responded that, well, he was a man.

Some men have an urgent need to preserve sexual harassment as a prerogative because, they feel, their manliness is at stake. But theirs is just one definition of manliness—a toxic and outdated one. It's time to move on.

The Workplace Today

Virtually all women and most men are now aligned against that toxic brand of masculinity. No one is asking men to stop being men or for people to stop being sexual beings. What's happened is that a small group of men are being required to abandon the stereotype that "real men" need to be unrelentingly sexual without regard to context or consent.

The not-unreasonable assumption is that work relationships should be about work. Some organizations have no-dating policies for that reason. If yours doesn't, remember that you must not take a relationship with a colleague in a romantic or sexual direction if doing so is unwelcome. Whether you can ask a colleague out is the source of much anxiety, especially in all-consuming work environments where people date coworkers because they spend so much time on the job that there's little opportunity to meet anyone else.

The only way to safely tell what someone else wants is to ask that person. Some men seem to have trouble discerning whether a woman is interested; Charlie Rose and Glenn Thrush said that they thought their feelings were reciprocated when women who received their overtures say they were not. This is not an unsolvable problem. If she's a work colleague and you'd like her to be something more, here's what to do: Imagine telling a woman who's been your friend forever that you'd like to take the relationship in a different direction. Ask in a way that gives her a chance to say that she prefers to remain a friend. No harm, no foul. What if your work colleague says no when she really means yes? Well, then, she's got to live with that. Let her. Let her change her mind if she wants to.

We all know that deals and crucial networking happen over lunch, dinner, and drinks. Socializing in this manner is fine. But if you do socialize with work colleagues, you need to realize that you can't behave inappropriately. Roy Price resigned from his job as head of Amazon Studios after Isa Hackett, an Amazon producer, publicly accused him of repeatedly propositioning her in a cab on the way to a work party, telling her, "You'll love my dick," and later at the gathering whispering "anal sex" loudly in her ear in the presence of others. Hollywood commentator Nellie Andreeva noted that in a post-Weinstein world Price's behavior would have hurt Amazon's ability to attract female showrunners and actors. He would have been "completely ostracized," an anonymous source told Andreeva.

You can still compliment your colleagues. But there's a big difference between "I like that dress" and "You look hot in that dress." What if she really *does* look hot? Remember, she signed up to be your colleague, not your girlfriend. Treat her like a colleague unless by mutual consent, you change your relationship.

Don't let the pendulum swing too far the other way and bizarrely avoid women completely. That's unnecessary, unfair, and illegal: It deprives women of opportunities simply because they are women. You cannot refuse to have closed-door meetings with women unless you refuse to have closed-door meetings with men. Otherwise women will be denied access to all the sensitive information that's shared only behind closed doors, and that's a violation of federal law.

Moving forward, male allies will continue to play an important role in fighting harassment: If you see something, say something. It does take courage, but you can use a light touch. If you're standing around with a bunch of guys and a female colleague walks by, only to have someone say, "Wow, she's hot," you can say simply: "I don't think of her that way. I think of her as a colleague, and that's the way I suspect she'd like to be thought of."

Clear takeaways emerge for women, too. If a coworker tries to take a work relationship in a sexual direction, tell him clearly if that's unwelcome. If you face sexual joking that's making you uncomfortable, say, "This is making me uncomfortable" and expect it to stop. If you want to shame or jolly someone out of misbehavior while preserving your business relationships, consult Joan's *What Works for Women at Work*. Here's an approach that worked for one woman whose colleague proposed an affair: "I know your wife. She's my friend. You're married. There is just no way I would ever consider that. So let's not go there again."

But it's our final piece of advice that signals the tectonic shift: If you are being sexually harassed, report it. We're not sure if we would have advised that, in such a blanket and unnuanced way, even a year ago.

What we're seeing today is not the end of sex, or of seduction, or of *la différence*. What we're seeing is the demise of a work culture where women must submit to being treated, insistently and incessantly, as sexual opportunities. Most people, when they go to work, want to work. And now they can.

How Do Your Workers Feel About Harassment? Ask Them

by Andrea S. Kramer and Alton B. Harris

If your business is serious about eliminating the risk of sexual harassment—and it should be—you need to approach the problem comprehensively. This means recognizing that sexual harassment is part of a continuum of interconnected behaviors that range from gender bias to incivility to legally actionable assault. All these kinds of misconduct should be addressed collectively, because sexual harassment is far more likely in organizations that experience offenses on the "less severe" end of the spectrum than in those that don't.

There's no one-size-fits-all program for eliminating inappropriate gender-related behaviors; the best programs specifically address the characteristics of each workplace's culture. The vital first step, then, is to get an accurate picture of yours. How? Ask your employees directly. Do they see disparities in career opportunities? Are colleagues or supervisors rude to each other? Is there inappropriate sexual conduct? Do employees feel uncomfortable or unsafe at work?

The best way to find all this out is with a carefully designed employee survey. In this article we'll offer some key principles for fashioning one, along with a model survey that you can adapt (which incorporates some of the recommendations the EEOC made for surveys in its 2017 proposed enforcement guidance on harassment). Our advice is based on insights we developed while working with major business organizations and conducting several hundred gender-focused workshops and moderated conversations around the United States.

Though we think a workplace climate survey can be immensely valuable, we caution that managers and leaders should proceed only if they're fully committed to thoroughly and quickly addressing inappropriate behavior in their organizations. Once the surveys are undertaken, they'll create expectations of remedial action. They might also attract unwanted publicity or be used against the company in future litigation. Those risks, however, are substantially outweighed by the opportunity to develop a work environment that's free of sexual misconduct, gender bias, and incivility.

Step 1: Communicate with Employees

Inform your employees that you're undertaking an effort to understand how fair, courteous, and safe their workplace is. The goal is to encourage engaged and completely candid answers to the survey. For that reason, it should be anonymous and administered by a third party, not your HR department. Employees won't have faith that their answers are confidential if the survey is conducted in-house, and if you don't offer true anonymity, their responses are less likely to be honest.

It's crucial for employees to believe that management considers an unbiased and harassment-free workplace a priority and is sincere in its commitment to that objective. That will happen only if senior management openly endorses the initiative, communicates the importance of supporting it to the entire management team, and periodically speaks to all employees about it.

Employees also need to believe that the end result will be better policies for everyone. This last point can't be emphasized too strongly. If the steps you take to combat inappropriate gender-related behaviors are seen solely as efforts to "protect" women because of their vulnerability, the initiative will backfire.

The first organization-wide letter to employees might begin with a statement like this:

We are gathering information on a confidential basis to better understand our business's workplace climate. Our goal is to ensure that all employees receive equal opportunities, respect, and resources in a workplace that is free of incivility and does not tolerate inappropriate sexual conduct.

The survey that you'll receive shortly is the first step toward achieving that objective.

We have hired a third-party administrator to conduct the survey on a strictly anonymous basis. Your answers and identity will be carefully protected from disclosure.

The administrator will contact you separately and detail its procedures for preserving anonymity.

The survey you'll receive is divided into four parts: gender bias, incivility, inappropriate sexual conduct, and overall workplace climate. All four areas are important, so please be as candid as possible in giving your views.

Employees should also be told that only the third-party administrator will see the raw survey results and that it will provide an analysis of those results to management. Once management receives that report, employees should be advised of the nature of and timetable for next steps.

We suggest that you emphasize that because the survey is anonymous, your organization cannot investigate or remedy specific claims raised by respondents—unless the incidents are separately reported in accordance with existing company procedures. Urge your employees to use those procedures if appropriate.

Step 2: Draw Up Your Survey

Whether you start with the assessment that we provide in this article or create your own questions, you should tailor your survey to your organization's culture and climate. Keep in mind the following:

- Avoid questions that could be used—or thought to be used—to identify participants, such as those about title, age, tenure with the company, responsibilities, and workplace location.

- Don't ask about marital or domestic status, sexual preference, children, or prior involvement in sexual misconduct investigations or proceedings. An inappropriate question in a job interview is equally inappropriate in a workplace climate survey.

- Keep the survey on point. Resist the temptation to use it as an opportunity to ask employees more broadly about their experiences, expectations, and future plans.

- Make the survey short and unambiguous. It should take no more than 10 minutes to finish. You may use true/false, multiple choice, or open-ended questions, but in our experience, the most useful approach is to incorporate a scale. Develop a series of statements that participants will be asked to indicate their degree of agreement with, using a scale of 1 (strongly disagree) to 7 (strongly agree). With statements that are intended to examine the frequency of specific behaviors, use a scale of 1 (very frequently) to 4 (never).

Step 3: Evaluate

A workplace climate survey needs no statistical evaluation beyond a simple tabulation. You're just attempting to determine whether some of your employees believe there are gender-related problems in your work environment and what those problems are.

Bear in mind that the survey is not an end in itself; it's a tool to identify whether you need new policies, practices, and procedures to eliminate inappropriate behavior and protect your employees against sexual harassment. Your results may indicate additional steps are necessary. You might need to assemble focus groups, conduct personal interviews, or host roundtable discussions. Since your goal is to ensure you have a welcoming, supportive, and productive workplace, the real work begins once you have a clear picture of your business's actual climate. Below is a template you can use when constructing your survey:

Model Workplace Climate Survey

Complete the following survey about your experience at XYZ Company, without referring to experiences at any prior organizations. The value of this survey depends directly on getting an accurate view of our workplace culture, so please answer all questions as honestly as possible.

1. Which of the following describes your gender?
   - Male
   - Female
   - Prefer to self-describe (specify)
   - Prefer not to say

Gender Bias

2. I feel valued by the organization.
   (1) Strongly disagree
   (2) Disagree
   (3) Slightly disagree
   (4) Neither agree nor disagree, or have no opinion
   (5) Slightly agree
   (6) Agree
   (7) Strongly agree

3. I believe my opportunities for career success are negatively affected by my gender.
   (1) Strongly disagree
   (2) Disagree
   (3) Slightly disagree
   (4) Neither agree nor disagree, or have no opinion
   (5) Slightly agree
   (6) Agree
   (7) Strongly agree

4. The people I work with treat me with respect and appreciation.
   (1) Strongly disagree
   (2) Disagree
   (3) Slightly disagree
   (4) Neither agree nor disagree, or have no opinion
   (5) Slightly agree
   (6) Agree
   (7) Strongly agree

5. My views are encouraged and welcomed by my supervisors and senior leaders without regard to my gender.
   (1) Strongly disagree
   (2) Disagree
   (3) Slightly disagree
   (4) Neither agree nor disagree, or have no opinion
   (5) Slightly agree
   (6) Agree
   (7) Strongly agree

6. Career-enhancing assignments and opportunities are disproportionately given to men.
   (1) Strongly disagree
   (2) Disagree
   (3) Slightly disagree
   (4) Neither agree nor disagree, or have no opinion
   (5) Slightly agree
   (6) Agree
   (7) Strongly agree

Civility

7. My coworkers are courteous and friendly.
   (1) Strongly disagree
   (2) Disagree
   (3) Slightly disagree
   (4) Neither agree nor disagree, or have no opinion

(5) Slightly agree
(6) Agree
(7) Strongly agree

8. I'm aware of unpleasant and negative gossip in the workplace.
   (1) Strongly disagree
   (2) Disagree
   (3) Slightly disagree
   (4) Neither agree nor disagree, or have no opinion
   (5) Slightly agree
   (6) Agree
   (7) Strongly agree

9. I'm aware of abusive, disrespectful, or hostile treatment of employees.
   (1) Strongly disagree
   (2) Disagree
   (3) Slightly disagree
   (4) Neither agree nor disagree, or have no opinion
   (5) Slightly agree
   (6) Agree
   (7) Strongly agree

10. I'm aware of bullying behavior in the workplace.
    (1) Strongly disagree
    (2) Disagree
    (3) Slightly disagree
    (4) Neither agree nor disagree, or have no opinion
    (5) Slightly agree
    (6) Agree
    (7) Strongly agree

11. There are adverse consequences for senior leaders who are abusive, disrespectful, or hostile.
    (1) Strongly disagree
    (2) Disagree
    (3) Slightly disagree
    (4) Neither agree nor disagree, or have no opinion
    (5) Slightly agree
    (6) Agree
    (7) Strongly agree

12. I have been criticized for my personal communication style or appearance.
    (1) Very frequently
    (2) Somewhat frequently
    (3) Not at all frequently
    (4) Never

13. All individuals are valued here.
    (1) Strongly disagree
    (2) Disagree
    (3) Slightly disagree
    (4) Neither agree nor disagree, or have no opinion
    (5) Slightly agree
    (6) Agree
    (7) Strongly agree

Inappropriate Sexual Conduct

14. I have experienced or witnessed unwanted physical conduct in the workplace or by coworkers away from the workplace.
    (1) Very frequently
    (2) Somewhat frequently
    (3) Not at all frequently
    (4) Never

15. I have witnessed or heard of offensive or inappropriate sexual jokes, innuendoes, banter, or comments in our workplace.
    (1) Very frequently
    (2) Somewhat frequently
    (3) Not at all frequently
    (4) Never

16. I have witnessed or heard of the electronic transmission of sexually explicit materials or comments by coworkers.
    (1) Very frequently
    (2) Somewhat frequently
    (3) Not at all frequently
    (4) Never

17. I have received sexually inappropriate phone calls, text messages, or social media attention from a coworker.
    (1) Very frequently
    (2) Somewhat frequently
    (3) Not at all frequently
    (4) Never

18. I have been asked or have witnessed inappropriate questions of a sexual nature.
    (1) Very frequently
    (2) Somewhat frequently
    (3) Not at all frequently
    (4) Never

19. I have been the subject of conduct that I consider to be sexual harassment.
    (1) Very frequently
    (2) Somewhat frequently

(3) Not at all frequently
(4) Never

20. Managers here tolerate or turn a blind eye to inappropriate sexual conduct.
    (1) Strongly disagree
    (2) Disagree
    (3) Slightly disagree
    (4) Neither agree nor disagree, or have no opinion
    (5) Slightly agree
    (6) Agree
    (7) Strongly agree

21. I feel unsafe at work because of inappropriate sexual conduct by some individuals.
    (1) Strongly disagree
    (2) Disagree
    (3) Slightly disagree
    (4) Neither agree nor disagree, or have no opinion
    (5) Slightly agree
    (6) Agree
    (7) Strongly agree

22. I've seen career opportunities be favorably allocated on the basis of existing or expected sexual interactions.
    (1) Strongly disagree
    (2) Disagree
    (3) Slightly disagree
    (4) Neither agree nor disagree, or have no opinion
    (5) Slightly agree
    (6) Agree
    (7) Strongly agree

23. I would be comfortable reporting inappropriate sexual conduct by a coworker.
    (1) Strongly disagree
    (2) Disagree
    (3) Slightly disagree
    (4) Neither agree nor disagree, or have no opinion
    (5) Slightly agree
    (6) Agree
    (7) Strongly agree

24. I would be comfortable reporting inappropriate sexual conduct by a supervisor.
    (1) Strongly disagree
    (2) Disagree
    (3) Slightly disagree

(4) Neither agree nor disagree, or have no opinion
(5) Slightly agree
(6) Agree
(7) Strongly agree

Overall Workplace Climate

25. My productivity has been affected by inappropriate gender-related behavior in the workplace.
    (1) Strongly disagree
    (2) Disagree
    (3) Slightly disagree
    (4) Neither agree nor disagree, or have no opinion
    (5) Slightly agree
    (6) Agree
    (7) Strongly agree

26. I have considered leaving my job because of inappropriate gender-related behavior in the workplace.
    (1) Strongly disagree
    (2) Disagree
    (3) Slightly disagree
    (4) Neither agree nor disagree, or have no opinion
    (5) Slightly agree
    (6) Agree
    (7) Strongly agree

27. Star performers are held to the same standards as other employees with respect to inappropriate gender-related behavior.
    (1) Strongly disagree
    (2) Disagree
    (3) Slightly disagree
    (4) Neither agree nor disagree, or have no opinion
    (5) Slightly agree
    (6) Agree
    (7) Strongly agree

28. I have experienced or witnessed inappropriate gender-related behavior by third parties (such as customers, vendors, and suppliers) associated with our organization.
    (1) Very frequently
    (2) Somewhat frequently
    (3) Not at all frequently
    (4) Never

29. The organization's policies and processes with respect to prohibiting and reporting inappropriate gender-related behavior are easy to understand and follow.
    (1) Strongly disagree
    (2) Disagree
    (3) Slightly disagree
    (4) Neither agree nor disagree, or have no opinion
    (5) Slightly agree
    (6) Agree
    (7) Strongly agree

Who's Harassed, and How?

by Heather McLaughlin

Imagine 100 young women. How many do you think will be sexually harassed by the age of 31?

Don't think just of the cases you've heard about in the news. Yes, the allegations about Harvey Weinstein, Roger Ailes, Charlie Rose, Matt Lauer, and many other famous and powerful men are disturbing, but the wave of revelations that followed are just as important. Thousands more women have broken their silence and publicly shared their #MeToo stories. It's now clear that sexual harassment is experienced by police officers, construction workers, accountants, kindergarten teachers, and workers in every occupation and industry around the world.

So, again, how many of those 100 women will be sexually harassed by age 31? At least 46%.

Is that figure surprising? Higher than you thought? Lower? One of the pernicious aspects of harassment is the difficulty of knowing precisely what's going on, how much it's going on, and who's doing it. I suspect the number is actually higher than this because of the nature of data collection and the fact that harassment is highly underreported, as I'll explore in this article. But data sets on it do exist. And the data we have puts the number at 46%.

That figure and the statistics in the following charts come from the Youth Development Study, which surveyed more than 1,000 individuals—both men and women—from St. Paul, Minnesota, from their freshman year in high school until their late thirties. Questions about sexual harassment were included in the surveys that participants took three times: when they were age 25 to 26, age 29 to 30, and age 30 to 31. The effort was the most comprehensive examination of workplace sexual harassment ever done in a longitudinal study, despite its geographic confines. Here are some of its findings:

Prevalence of Harassment

By their mid-twenties, one in three women had been sexually harassed, and as they grew older, that figure progressively rose, to nearly one in two. The latter two surveys asked just whether the women had experienced sexual harassment within the past year. I can safely project that if the data covered all the years in the women's late twenties or their entire lifetimes, the rate would be higher still.

Percentage of women who have experienced sexual harassment

At three different ages

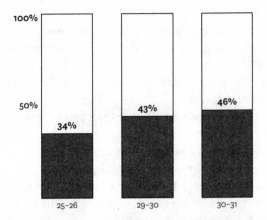

Note: Estimates include only women who responded to all three waves of data collection.

Behaviors Endured

When respondents were 30 to 31 years old, they were asked if they had experienced one or more harassing behaviors in the past year. More than one-third of women said they had. The more severe a behavior was, the less frequent it tended to be; leering was more common, for instance, than unwanted touching. But the numbers on all types of behaviors were astonishingly high for a one-year period.

Percentage of women experiencing one or more harassing behaviors within a single year

Percentage of women experiencing harassing behaviors

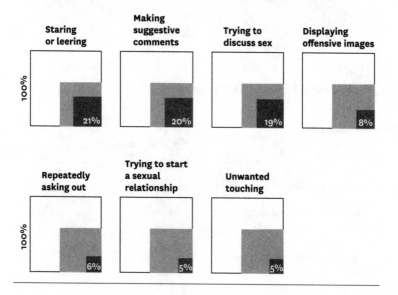

Power Dynamics

The typical harassment scenario we see in the news involves a clear organizational power dynamic: boss and subordinate. So it may surprise some people to learn that most harassment involves a lateral relationship: a coworker who doesn't officially have power over the target. Harassment is still a crime rooted in power, but it's important to look at lateral dynamics to understand who's harassing women woman and how.

Harassers' work relationship to targets

Of the nearly 400 harassers reported by women in one analysis, coworkers were responsible for three times more reported incidents than supervisors.

Frequency of types of harassment

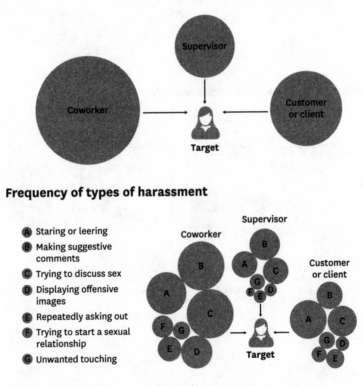

- **A** Staring or leering
- **B** Making suggestive comments
- **C** Trying to discuss sex
- **D** Displaying offensive images
- **E** Repeatedly asking out
- **F** Trying to start a sexual relationship
- **G** Unwanted touching

Note: Respondents could report more than one harasser.

Frequency

Sexual harassment at work is far from an isolated experience. The regularity of these incidents makes it evident that a larger culture of harassment exists; it's not just a few bad apples who are abusing their power. The data from the survey of respondents at age 30 to 31 shows that more targets endured multiple instances of harassing behaviors than experienced a single incident. This was true across every type of harassment.

Most harassing behaviors occur multiple times per year

Percentage of harassed women who said they experienced the behaviors:

Percentage of harassed women experiencing behavior

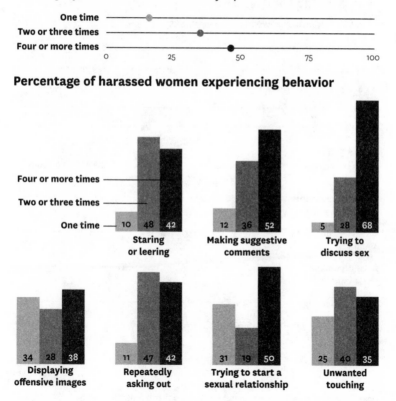

	Staring or leering	Making suggestive comments	Trying to discuss sex
One time	10	12	5
Two or three times	48	36	28
Four or more times	42	52	68

	Displaying offensive images	Repeatedly asking out	Trying to start a sexual relationship	Unwanted touching
	34	11	31	25
	28	47	19	40
	38	42	50	35

Note: May not add up to 100% because of rounding.

Underreporting

Some people have expressed skepticism about the recent wave of harassment claims, questioning why women didn't come forward sooner. But the data—in this case from the survey taken when respondents were 29 to 30—supports the assertion that many are harassed but few report it.

If targets told anyone at all, they tended to confide in a colleague or friend rather than someone in a position to address the problem.

(Note that the list of harassing behaviors differs slightly here because of survey design changes in the year this was asked.)

Who is notified of harassment

Percentage of harassed women who informed:

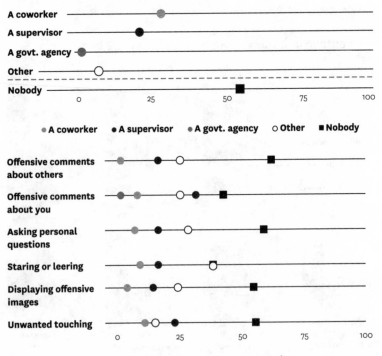

Note: Respondents could report harassment to more than one person/agency.

The many reasons that harassment goes unreported have been deeply explored. But one surprising reason may be that targets do not recognize some experiences as harassment, despite disliking them. A surprisingly low percentage of people who said they'd endured harassing behaviors at age 30 to 31 perceived them to be actual harassment.

Gender differences in experiences of sexual harassment

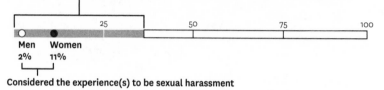

Percentage of people who experienced one or more sexually harassing behaviors: 36%

Men 2% Women 11%

Considered the experience(s) to be sexual harassment

Even those who experienced repeated harassment often downplayed the seriousness or inappropriateness of some interactions. The numbers indicate that this may be especially true for men. At the same time, women often experience behaviors like catcalling and other inappropriate comments and gestures in settings besides work, which may account for why many don't label them an illegal form of discrimination when they occur on the job. Perhaps more would now, in this particular cultural moment, but that is a question researchers have yet to answer. While it seems as if attitudes about what constitutes harassment and cultural acceptance of speaking out about it are changing, we won't know for sure if this is a permanent shift until several more years of data are collected.

It will be crucial to build on this data with follow-up questions in upcoming surveys to see if the dynamic shifts. If this extraordinary moment actually ushers in a new cultural norm and systemic changes, there should be a dramatic drop in the number of cases that go unreported and a significant rise in the percentage of people characterizing the behavior they endure as harassment. Organizations must change, as the costs of sexual harassment are high to both targets and their employers. *Time* magazine named the silence breakers the 2017 Person of the Year. Perhaps 2018 will be dedicated to the change makers.

Originally published in January 2018. Reprint BG1801

The Battle for Female Talent in Emerging Markets

by Sylvia Ann Hewlett and Ripa Rashid

AFTER WORKING FOR ALMOST 20 YEARS outside China at a global consulting firm, a woman we'll call Mei was recently forced to return home to Beijing, where she faces work/life pressures unrelated to raising children. Mei's elders needed care, and in China a social stigma is attached to using professional help or placing parents in assisted-living facilities. Mei worries about how these obligations will affect her career. Apart from facilitating her return home, however, the firm seems to be unaware of Mei's problems.

In the United Arab Emirates a rising star we'll call Rana is an analyst in the fixed-income division of a bank. Her company regularly offers opportunities for professional development, but Rana had to decline an invitation to a recent training session in New York, because a single woman from the UAE can't board a plane or stay in a hotel unless a male relative is willing to tag along. Adding insult to injury, no video hookup was provided to allow Rana to participate from home.

In many emerging markets, workplace bias seems to escalate for young mothers, who are under constant scrutiny. In India these women commonly return to less-challenging roles or projects or get lower performance ratings. A Brazilian woman told us about a colleague who was fired after being overheard mentioning plans to have a second child. Such explicitly discriminatory behaviors, although they violate company policies, continue unchecked.

Women in these countries face unique challenges, as the stories above show. This presents a major problem for multinational companies whose hopes for growth are pinned on emerging markets. They face a cutthroat war for talent, despite the enormous labor forces of the BRIC countries. India produces as many young engineers as the United States, and Russia produces 10 times as many finance and accounting professionals as Germany. Yet according to the McKinsey Global Institute, a mere 25% of those professionals in India and 20% in Russia are suitable for employment by multinationals. In China less than a 10th of university graduates are prepared to succeed in those organizations.

To meet the talent shortage in emerging markets, multinationals often send managers overseas (not a sustainable solution) or compete with local companies. They need to develop the best-educated and best-prepared managers in those markets, which increasingly means women. Every year large numbers of college-educated women enter the BRIC professional workforce; in 2006 the number was around 26 million. Furthermore, these women are highly ambitious. As we will show, smart multinationals recognize their potential and have found ways to recruit and retain them, giving them the support they need to break through a very thick glass ceiling.

The Talent

To bring these practices to light, we launched a study (the first of its kind) of talent in emerging economies. The study was spearheaded by five global companies that are grappling with the complex challenges associated with globalization: Bloomberg, Booz & Company, Intel, Pfizer, and Siemens. We collected data on 4,350 college-educated men and women in Brazil, Russia, India, China, and the United Arab Emirates, and supplemented them with qualitative research from focus groups, virtual strategy sessions, and interviews with hundreds of white-collar women. Western media often focus on stereotypical images of deprived and oppressed women in less-developed countries, overlooking this vibrant and growing segment of the population. We found that talented women in emerging markets are ahead of the curve in unexpected ways.

Education

Our most surprising finding is that women are flooding into universities and graduate schools: They represent 65% of college graduates in the UAE, 60% in Brazil, and 47% in China. In Russia, where communism promoted universal access to education, 86% of women aged 18 to 23 are enrolled in tertiary education. More than a third in that age group are enrolled in tertiary education in Brazil and the UAE, and 50% of the Indian women (versus 40% of the Indian men) in our sample hold graduate degrees.

Ambition

Although highly educated women the world over are ambitious, the degree of ambition and aspiration among BRIC and UAE women is extraordinary: 85% in India and 92% in the UAE consider themselves very ambitious, and in Russia and China the figures are 63% and 65%, respectively. (Only 36% of U.S. women consider themselves

---

Women with ambition

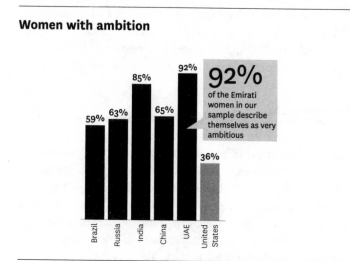

92% of the Emirati women in our sample describe themselves as very ambitious

Brazil 59% · Russia 63% · India 85% · China 65% · UAE 92% · United States 36%

---

very ambitious.) Furthermore, 80% or more of women in Brazil, India, and the UAE aspire to hold a top job.

Commitment

More than 80% of respondents in Brazil, Russia, India, and the UAE report loving their work, and a similarly high percentage are "willing to go the extra mile" for their companies. This is good news for employers, particularly in light of a 2007–2008 Towers Perrin finding that a mere 21% of global workers are engaged in their work. BRIC and UAE women express a deep connection to and passion for their jobs, citing intellectual stimulation, a sense of personal growth, and the quality of colleagues as key motivators—on a par with job security and compensation. Underlying these factors is the satisfaction of being part of the emerging-market success story. As Leila Hoteit, a UAE-based principal at Booz & Company, puts it, "We have the opportunity to be involved in high-impact projects that are reshaping countries and the region as a whole."

The Problem

Unfortunately, female talent is underleveraged in emerging markets. Part of the reason is that family-related pulls and work-related pushes conspire to force women to either settle for dead-end jobs or leave the workforce. The inducements to languish or leave reflect both entrenched cultural perspectives and modern complexities.

Elder care

As we saw with Mei, family-rooted pulls come from a direction that companies might not expect: the older generation. Professional women in BRIC and the UAE are less encumbered than women elsewhere by child-care issues, because many grandparents are active caregivers (cultural visions of old-age pursuits center more on family than on individual leisure), and working mothers have access to affordable domestic help and a growing infrastructure of day-care and early-childhood centers. But in India and China notions of filial piety underpin the cultural value system; although many women in

Women's income

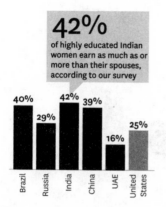

42%
of highly educated Indian women earn as much as or more than their spouses, according to our survey

40% 29% 42% 39% 16% 25%

Brazil Russia India China UAE United States

our sample had no children, 70% or more had elder-care responsibilities. In some countries daughterly guilt—and its alternative, daughterly responsibility—are an even greater burden than maternal guilt.

Far more adult women in BRIC and the UAE than in the U.S. live with their parents or in-laws. From 40% to 68% also assist their parents financially, providing 18% to 23% of their elders' income—necessary in countries where state benefits for the elderly are limited or nonexistent. As a highly qualified Emirati woman explained to us, "It is part of the expectation of what children do in the Arab world. We take care of our parents when we grow up."

The lure of the public sector

Family-friendly jobs in the public sector are another oft-ignored pull. More than half our respondents in Brazil, India, and China consider the public sector "very desirable," citing job security, professional opportunities, benefits, and prestige. In the UAE public-sector salaries are equal to or higher than private-sector ones, so Emiratis account for less than 1% of private-sector staff but 54% of employees in federal ministries. A recent Indian study of men and women students found that 60% aspire to public-sector positions over private-sector ones.

Perceived gender discrimination

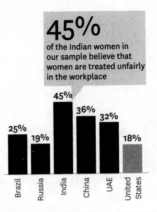

45%
of the Indian women in our sample believe that women are treated unfairly in the workplace

45%

36%

32%

25%

19%

18%

Brazil Russia India China UAE United States

Powerful gender bias

In BRIC and the UAE professional women face a triple whammy of gender, ethnicity, and cultural attitudes. Of our respondents in Brazil, China, and the UAE, 25% to 36% believe that women are treated unfairly in the workplace because of their gender; in India the number is 45%. In Russia the figure is only 19%, again owing to its communist legacy.

Travel and safety

Social disapproval of women traveling alone is strong in many societies, with more than half our survey respondents in India and China citing difficulties. This puts industries and corporate positions that require travel at a disadvantage in attracting and retaining talented women. Sales roles in India's pharmaceutical sector, for example, involve frequent trips to semiurban and rural locations, so recruiting women for them is a challenge. The same is true in the industrial and infrastructure sectors. Women often concentrate on careers with local responsibilities—such as medicine, law, hotel administration, advertising, public relations, nursing, and education—or gravitate toward finance and the media, which are city-based and require minimal travel. But even an urban context can be daunting for women. Economic shifts aside, mass culture in India remains tradition-bound and male-dominated. In 2009 commuter trains exclusively for female passengers—Ladies Specials—were introduced in Mumbai, New Delhi, Chennai, and Calcutta to provide a safe haven from the harassment women face when using public transportation.

Other safety concerns are a harsh reality for professional women in emerging markets. In Russia crime is escalating: In one month in 2009 Moscow's murder rate rose by 16% and its fatal assaults by 44%. According to a recent U.S. State Department report, "Assaults and burglaries continue to be a part of normal everyday life" in São Paolo and Rio de Janeiro. Rape cases in India rose by more than 30% from 2003 to 2007, and kidnapping or abduction cases rose by more than 50%. These dangers strongly influence women's preferences about what type of career to pursue.

How to Attract and Keep Talented Women

The opportunity has never been greater for multinationals to attract and retain top talent in emerging economies. For some it's an imperative. Melinda Wolfe, Bloomberg's head of professional development, says, "Bloomberg is now in 146 countries and growing at a rapid pace. We have an urgent need to draw upon a deep pool of local talent—both men and women—to deliver excellence." Forward-thinking companies can do several things to maximize the opportunity.

Find talent early

With so many women earning advanced degrees throughout the developing world, the best place to start looking for talent is the universities. Smart companies adopt a creative and targeted approach, differentiating their brand as employers of choice for talented women. For example, the Google India Women in Engineering Award was launched in 2008 to celebrate women pursuing engineering and computer sciences careers in college or graduate school. Sixteen women in 2008 and nine in 2009 won the $2,000 award; Google senior managers and engineers serve as judges. Anjali Sardana, a

The Top-Talent Pool

PERCENTAGE OF COLLEGE GRADUATES in 2007 who were women:

UAE **65%**

Brazil **60%**

United States **58%**

China **47%**

---

doctoral candidate at the Indian Institute of Technology (Roorkee), a 2009 winner from among 250 applicants, says that the award has inspired her to keep pursuing her dreams: "Not only did the award encourage me to stay in my field, it has made me confident and given me the spark to mentor other, younger women engineers."

Help them build networks

Ensuring that top talent in emerging markets feels valued is of fundamental importance in multinational organizations, particularly those headquartered in the U.S. or Western Europe. Networking and relationship building, essential to strengthening engagement and commitment, help women develop the ties, visibility, and organizational know-how essential to professional success. Siemens launched a program this year to establish a network for its young, high-potential managers in emerging markets. The company invites them to develop business-centered projects that will contribute to its success; the first plans were presented to Siemens leadership in the spring of 2010.

Smart companies are using networks to help women fight isolation and gain visibility as well as achieve their business goals. For instance, General Electric is piloting a version of its myConnections talent-spotting and mentoring program in the UAE. Its goal is to help women connect with one another across levels and functions in the company, recognizing how critical relationships are to career success. The program has been opened up to all of GE's female employees in the UAE. Participants are sorted into "pods" of 10 to 12 members each and assigned a coach, typically a rising female star on the verge of becoming a leader; they determine their own agendas. Four pods

Women's Hours at Work

IN THE COUNTRIES WE STUDIED, educated women working full time at multinational companies say they put in significantly more than 40 hours a week, on average.

73 hours in Russia

71 hours in China

58 hours in India

53 hours in the UAE

49 hours in Brazil

have been launched. At one kickoff meeting a woman said that she worked in finance but was based across town from most of her colleagues and felt she was missing out. "I can help you," said another participant, the executive assistant to the region's chief financial officer. As a result, the frustrated finance employee met a senior female finance leader and started building closer ties with her department.

Similarly, Women at Intel Network (WIN) in China, an extension of a global program initiated 13 years ago, endeavors to strike a balance between global goals—in areas ranging from membership to professional development—and local priorities and cultural contexts. In 2007 Intel China became the first to initiate a chapter outside the U.S.; it now has groups in Chengdu, Shanghai, Beijing, and Dalian. "It's not easy for women to have a role in this industry," says Helen Tian, the operations manager of Intel China Research Center and a cohead of the Beijing chapter of WIN. "WIN can bring our women a lot of inspiration to share ideas and help each other on career development."

At monthly meetings the local chapters host visiting senior American women who offer key advice to their Chinese counterparts. For instance, a session on leadership skills and career development in challenging times encouraged women to take on stretch assignments or cross-train with coworkers. In the spring of 2008 Tian helped organize the first Chinese WIN Leadership Development Conference, bringing 300 Intel women together in Shanghai to attend sessions on work/life balance, stress, and technical skills.

How to Attract and Keep Talented Women

1. Find talent early. The best place to start looking is in the universities.

2. Help your women recruits build networks to fight isolation and gain visibility while achieving their business goals.

3. Give them international exposure, but provide plenty of support for families in the host countries.

4. Build ties outside the company—to clients, customers, and communities.

Give them international exposure

Women are more likely to break through the glass ceiling in multinational companies that make sure they are posted overseas for short periods. However, in emerging markets these assignments work best when companies can provide flexibility and support to lighten the burden on spouses and families. For instance, the German pharmaceutical giant Boehringer Ingelheim has a short-term assignment program that enables less-mobile employees to gain international exposure. Its assignments—offered around the globe, with a current focus on the Americas—last three to six months and provide development opportunities for high-potential directors and managers. Boehringer Ingelheim supplies housing and transportation in the host country, along with support for family members, including child care, elder care, paid monthly visits for spouses, or opportunities for family members to come along for the entire stay. When a woman from Venezuela took an assignment to Ecuador, Boehringer Ingelheim sent her mother along, too. One woman's stay-at-home husband went with her on assignment to Latin America.

Build communities outside the company

Maximizing opportunities within the company produces great results for professional women, but it's also important to help them build ties to their clients, customers, and communities in emerging markets. These external networks serve two purposes: One is to establish a broader support system for women who are navigating pushes and pulls—particularly important when they have few role models at the top. The other is to strengthen the relationships that help them achieve business results.

The global pharmaceutical giant Pfizer has made it a business priority to engage and retain high-potential female talent in India— one of its top growth markets. The company recently piloted Creating a High Performance Community, under the guidance of its Global Women's Council. The program has three main goals: to ensure that top female talent feels valued and supported; to strengthen connections among Pfizer's high-performing women and their women customers; and to test an approach potentially useful in other markets.

As a starting point, Pfizer India identified its top 10 women in sales and marketing and its 10 most important women customers (including physicians in private practice, medical professionals in high-profile hospitals, medical technologists, and so forth). The women participated in a focus group to discuss their career goals and the professional challenges and opportunities they faced. What emerged was a narrative of blazing ambition often blocked by cultural barriers. The women compared notes on the usual issues of work/life balance, but also on how their career aspirations ran contrary to societal expectations. The pilot has established a powerful forum in which Pfizer's rising stars can network with their customers—one where they can celebrate successes and compare difficulties, thus deepening relationships and combating the isolation so frequently experienced by women rising through the ranks. Pfizer India plans to hold a workshop this spring to provide essential career navigation and leadership development skills.

It will be years before the glass ceiling is broken in emerging markets, but some multinational companies are helping to speed up the process by ensuring that they attract and retain the most talented women available. This not only improves the prospects of these companies in developing countries but also has a significant effect on the women they employ. The remarkable reality is that these women are at the forefront of change, shaping the very world in which they live.

Originally published in May 2010. Reprint R1005H

Off-Ramps and On-Ramps

Keeping Talented Women on the
Road to Success. *by Sylvia Ann Hewlett
and Carolyn Buck Luce*

THROUGHOUT THE PAST YEAR, a noisy debate has erupted in the media over the meaning of what Lisa Belkin of the *New York Times* has called the "opt-out revolution." Recent articles in the *Wall Street Journal,* the *New York Times, Time,* and *Fast Company* all point to a disturbing trend—large numbers of highly qualified women dropping out of mainstream careers. These articles also speculate on what might be behind this new brain drain. Are the complex demands of modern child rearing the nub of the problem? Or should one blame the trend on a failure of female ambition?

The facts and figures in these articles are eye-catching: a survey of the class of 1981 at Stanford University showing that 57% of women graduates leave the work force; a survey of three graduating classes at Harvard Business School demonstrating that only 38% of women graduates end up in full-time careers; and a broader-gauged study of MBAs showing that one in three white women holding an MBA is not working full-time, compared with one in 20 for men with the same degree.

The stories that enliven these articles are also powerful: Brenda Barnes, the former CEO of PepsiCo, who gave up her megawatt career to spend more time with her three children; Karen Hughes, who resigned from her enormously influential job in the Bush White House to go home to Texas to better look after a needy teenage son;

and a raft of less prominent women who also said goodbye to their careers. Lisa Beattie Frelinghuysen, for example—featured in a recent *60 Minutes* segment—was building a very successful career as a lawyer. She'd been president of the law review at Stanford and went to work for a prestigious law firm. She quit after she had her first baby three years later.

These stories certainly resonate, but scratch the surface and it quickly becomes clear that there is very little in the way of systematic, rigorous data about the seeming exodus. A sector here, a graduating class there, and a flood of anecdotes: No one seems to know the basic facts. Across professions and across sectors, what is the scope of this opt-out phenomenon? What proportion of professional women take off-ramps rather than continue on their chosen career paths? Are they pushed off or pulled? Which sectors of the economy are most severely affected when women leave the workforce? How many years do women tend to spend out of the workforce? When women decide to reenter, what are they looking for? How easy is it to find on-ramps? What policies and practices help women return to work?

Early in 2004, the Center for Work-Life Policy formed a private sector, multiyear task force entitled "The Hidden Brain Drain: Women and Minorities as Unrealized Assets" to answer these and other questions. In the summer of 2004, three member companies of the task force (Ernst & Young, Goldman Sachs, and Lehman Brothers) sponsored a survey specifically designed to investigate the role of off-ramps and on-ramps in the lives of highly qualified women. The survey, conducted by Harris Interactive, comprised a nationally representative group of highly qualified women, defined as those with a graduate degree, a professional degree, or a high-honors undergraduate degree. The sample size was 2,443 women. The survey focused on two age groups: older women aged 41 to 55 and younger women aged 28 to 40. We also surveyed a smaller group of highly qualified men (653) to allow us to draw comparisons.

Using the data from the survey, we've created a more comprehensive and nuanced portrait of women's career paths than has been available to date. Even more important, these data suggest actions

Idea in Brief

For professional women, it's unusual *not* to step off the career fast track at least once. With children to raise, elderly parents to care for, and other family demands, many women feel they have little choice but to off-ramp.

When women are ready to step back on track, opportunities are limited: Available jobs don't measure up in pay or prestige to previous positions. Result? Women returning to the workforce are demoralized. And companies miss the chance to leverage women's best skills. With talent shortages looming over the next decade, firms must reverse the female brain drain if they hope to beat rivals.

Like it or not, many highly skilled women need to take time off. How to ensure your company's access to their talents over the long term? Help off-ramping women maintain connections that will enable them to reenter the workforce without being marginalized. Reduced-hour jobs, flexible workdays, and removal of off-ramping's stigma are just a few strategies. For example, consulting firm Ernst & Young used such approaches to reverse an expensive downward trend in women's retention and increase its percentage of female partners threefold.

that companies can take to ensure that female potential does not go unrealized. Given current demographic and labor market trends, it's imperative that employers learn to reverse this brain drain. Indeed, companies that can develop policies and practices to tap into the female talent pool over the long haul will enjoy a substantial competitive advantage.

Women Do Leave

Many women take an off-ramp at some point on their career highway. Nearly four in ten highly qualified women (37%) report that they have left work voluntarily at some point in their careers. Among women who have children, that statistic rises to 43%.

Factors other than having children that pull women away from their jobs include the demands of caring for elderly parents or other family members (reported by 24%) and personal health issues (9%). Not surprisingly, the pull of elder care responsibilities is particularly

Idea in Practice

How to reverse female brain drain in your firm? Consider these strategies:

Create Reduced-Hour Jobs

Offer women ways to keep a hand in their chosen field, short of full-time involvement.

> *Example:* By offering part-time schedules, consumer-products giant Johnson & Johnson boosted employee loyalty and productivity. Female part-time managers maintain they would have quit had part-time jobs not been available. Instead, they push themselves to perform at the same level they achieved before going part-time.

Provide Flexible Workdays

Offer variety in when, where, and how work gets done. A caregiver for an invalid or fragile elderly person may have many hours of potentially productive time in a day, yet not be able to stray far from home.

Provide Flexible Career Arcs

Offer alternative paths that support women during on-ramping and off-ramping phases—so they don't have to quit their career cold turkey.

> *Example:* Management consultancy Booz Allen Hamilton created a pilot "reserve" program for current employees and alumni. It "unbundled" standard management consulting work, identifying bite-sized chunks that could be done via telecommuting or short stints in the office. Then it created a standard employment contract

strong for women in the 41 to 55 age group—often called the "sandwich" generation, positioned as it is between growing children and aging parents. One in three women in that bracket have left work for some period to spend time caring for family members who are not children. And lurking behind all this is the pervasiveness of a highly traditional division of labor on the home front. In a 2001 survey conducted by the Center for Work-Life Policy, fully 40% of highly qualified women with spouses felt that their husbands create more work around the house than they perform.

Alongside these "pull" factors are a series of "push" factors—that is, features of the job or workplace that make women head for the door. Seventeen percent of women say they took an off-ramp, at least in part, because their jobs were not satisfying or meaningful. Overall, that's activated when chunks of part-time work become available. With 150 women employees operating under part-time employment contracts, the company has retained valuable female talent.

Remove the Stigma

Create policies that allow employees to adopt unconventional work arrangements without suffering damage to their careers.

Example: Ernst & Young's chairman made retaining and promoting women a priority. The company equipped all employees for telework and ensured that alternative work schedules didn't affect promotion opportunities. It also created a database of flexible work arrangements. Interested parties learn how arrangements are structured, contact participants with questions, and share lessons learned.

Stop Burning Bridges

Explore off-ramping women's reasons for departing, offering options short of total severance. Clarify that your company's door will remain open to them. And maintain connections with off-ramped employees through formal alumni programs.

Nurture Ambition

Establish "old girls" networks enabling women to build skills, contacts, and confidence, as well as earn recognition. You'll help them sustain their passion for work and their competitive edge.

understimulation and lack of opportunity seem to be larger problems than overwork. Only 6% of women stopped working because the work itself was too demanding. In business sectors, the survey results suggest that push factors are particularly powerful—indeed, in these sectors, unlike, say, in medicine or teaching, they outweigh pull factors. Of course, in the hurly-burly world of everyday life, most women are dealing with a combination of push and pull factors—and one often serves to intensify the other. When women feel hemmed in by rigid policies or a glass ceiling, for example, they are much more likely to respond to the pull of family.

It's important to note that, however pulled or pushed, only a relatively privileged group of women have the option of not working. Most women cannot quit their careers unless their spouses earn considerable incomes. Fully 32% of the women surveyed cite the fact that their spouses' income "was sufficient for our family to live on one income" as a reason contributing to their decision to off-ramp.

Contrast this with the experience of highly qualified men, only 24% of whom have taken off-ramps (with no statistical difference between those who are fathers and those who are not). When men leave the workforce, they do it for different reasons. Child-care and elder-care responsibilities are much less important; only 12% of men cite these factors as compared with 44% of women. Instead, on the pull side, they cite switching careers (29%), obtaining additional training (25%), or starting a business (12%) as important reasons for taking time out. For highly qualified men, off-ramping seems to be about strategic repositioning in their careers—a far cry from the dominant concerns of their female peers.

For many women in our study, the decision to off-ramp is a tough one. These women have invested heavily in their education and training. They have spent years accumulating the skills and credentials necessary for successful careers. Most are not eager to toss that painstaking effort aside.

Lost on Reentry

Among women who take off-ramps, the overwhelming majority have every intention of returning to the workforce—and seemingly little idea of just how difficult that will prove. Women, like lawyer Lisa Beattie Frelinghuysen from the *60 Minutes* segment, who happily give up their careers to have children are the exception rather than the rule. In our research, we find that most highly qualified women who are currently off-ramped (93%) want to return to their careers.

Many of these women have financial reasons for wanting to get back to work. Nearly half (46%) cite "having their own independent source of income" as an important propelling factor. Women who participated in focus groups conducted as part of our research talked about their discomfort with "dependence." However good

How Many Opt Out?

IN OUR SURVEY OF HIGHLY QUALIFIED PROFESSIONALS, we asked the question, "Since you first began working, has there ever been a period where you took a voluntary time out from work?" Nearly four in ten women reported that they had—and that statistic rises to 43% among women who have children. By contrast, only 24% of highly qualified men have taken off-ramps (with no statistical difference between those who are fathers and those who are not).

Women   Men

their marriages, many disliked needing to ask for money. Not being able to splurge on some small extravagance or make their own philanthropic choices without clearing it with their husbands did not sit well with them. It's also true that a significant proportion of women currently seeking on-ramps are facing troubling shortfalls in family income: 38% cite "household income no longer sufficient for family needs" and 24% cite "partner's income no longer sufficient for family needs." Given what has happened to the cost of homes (up 38% over the past five years), the cost of college education (up 40% over the past decade), and the cost of health insurance (up 49% since 2000), it's easy to see why many professional families find it hard to manage on one income.

But financial pressure does not tell the whole story. Many of these women find deep pleasure in their chosen careers and want to reconnect with something they love. Forty-three percent cite the "enjoyment and satisfaction" they derive from their careers as an important reason to return—among teachers this figure rises to 54% and among doctors it rises to 70%. A further 16% want to "regain power and status in their profession." In our focus groups, women talked eloquently about how work gives shape and structure to their lives, boosts confidence and self-esteem, and confers status and standing in their communities. For many off-rampers, their professional identities remain their primary identities, despite the fact that they have taken time out.

Perhaps most interesting, 24% of the women currently looking for on-ramps are motivated by "a desire to give something back to society" and are seeking jobs that allow them to contribute to their communities in some way. In our focus groups, off-ramped women talked about how their time at home had changed their aspirations. Whether they had gotten involved in protecting the wetlands, supporting the local library, or rebuilding a playground, they felt newly connected to the importance of what one woman called "the work of care."

Unfortunately, only 74% of off-ramped women who want to rejoin the ranks of the employed manage to do so, according to our survey. And among these, only 40% return to full-time, professional jobs. Many (24%) take part-time jobs, and some (9%) become self-employed. The implication is clear: Off-ramps are around every curve in the road, but once a woman has taken one, on-ramps are few and far between—and extremely costly.

The Penalties of Time Out

Women off-ramp for surprisingly short periods of time—on average, 2.2 years. In business sectors, off-rampers average even shorter periods of time out (1.2 years). However, even these relatively short career interruptions entail heavy financial penalties. Our data show that women lose an average of 18% of their earning power when they take an off-ramp. In business sectors, penalties are particularly draconian: In these fields, women's earning power dips an average of 28% when they take time out. The longer you spend out, the more severe the penalty becomes. Across sectors, women lose a staggering 37% of their earning power when they spend three or more years out of the workforce.

Naomi, 34, is a case in point. In an interview, this part-time working mother was open about her anxieties: "Every day, I think about what I am going to do when I want to return to work full-time. I worry about whether I will be employable—will anyone even look at

Why Do They Leave the Fast Lane?

OUR SURVEY DATA SHOW that women and men take off-ramps for dramatically different reasons. While men leave the workforce mainly to reposition themselves for a career change, the majority of women off-ramp to attend to responsibilities at home.

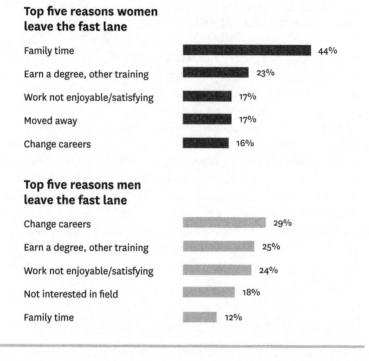

Top five reasons women leave the fast lane

Family time	44%
Earn a degree, other training	23%
Work not enjoyable/satisfying	17%
Moved away	17%
Change careers	16%

Top five reasons men leave the fast lane

Change careers	29%
Earn a degree, other training	25%
Work not enjoyable/satisfying	24%
Not interested in field	18%
Family time	12%

my résumé?" This is despite an MBA and substantial work experience.

Three years ago, Naomi felt she had no choice but to quit her lucrative position in market research. She had just had a child, and returning to full-time work after the standard maternity leave proved to be well-nigh impossible. Her 55-hour week combined with her husband's 80-hour week didn't leave enough time to raise a healthy child—let alone care for a child who was prone to illness, as theirs was. When her employer denied her request to work reduced hours, Naomi quit.

After nine months at home, Naomi did find some flexible work—but it came at a high price. Her new freelance job as a consultant to an advertising agency barely covered the cost of her son's day care. She now earns a third of what she did three years ago. What plagues Naomi the most about her situation is her anxiety about the future. "Will my skills become obsolete? Will I be able to support myself and my son if something should happen to my husband?"

The scholarly literature shows that Naomi's experience is not unusual. Economist Jane Waldfogel has analyzed the pattern of earnings over the life span. When women enter the workforce in their early and mid twenties they earn nearly as much as men do. For a few years, they almost keep pace. For example, at ages 25 to 29, they earn 87% of the male wage. However, when women start having children, their earnings fall way behind those of men. By the time they reach the 40-to-44 age group, women earn a mere 71% of the male wage. In the words of MIT economist Lester Thurow, "These are the prime years for establishing a successful career. These are the years when hard work has the maximum pay-off. They are also the prime years for launching a family. Women who leave the job market during those years may find that they never catch up."

Taking the Scenic Route

A majority (58%) of highly qualified women describe their careers as "nonlinear"—which is to say, they do not follow the conventional trajectory long established by successful men. That ladder of success features a steep gradient in one's 30s and steady progress thereafter. In contrast, these women report that their "career paths have not followed a progression through the hierarchy of an industry."

Some of this nonlinearity is the result of taking off-ramps. But there are many other ways in which women ease out of the professional fast lane. Our survey reveals that 16% of highly qualified women work part-time. Such arrangements are more prevalent in the legal and medical professions, where 23% and 20% of female

The High Cost of Time Out

THOUGH THE AVERAGE AMOUNT of time that women take off from their careers is surprisingly short (less than three years), the salary penalty for doing so is severe. Women who return to the workforce after time out earn significantly less than their peers who remained in their jobs.

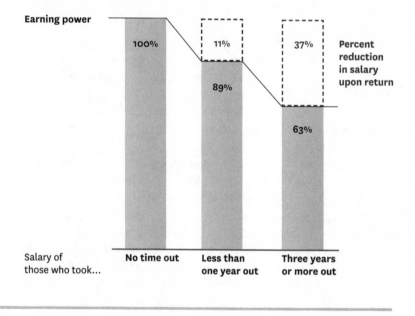

Earning power

| 100% | 11% | 37% | Percent reduction in salary upon return |

89%

63%

Salary of those who took... **No time out** | **Less than one year out** | **Three years or more out**

professionals work less than full-time, than in the business sector, where only 8% of women work part-time. Another common work-life strategy is telecommuting; 8% of highly qualified women work exclusively from home, and another 25% work partly from home.

Looking back over their careers, 36% of highly qualified women say they have worked part-time for some period of time as part of a strategy to balance work and personal life. Twenty-five percent say they have reduced the number of work hours within a full-time job, and 16% say they have declined a promotion. A significant proportion (38%) say they have deliberately chosen a position with fewer responsibilities and lower compensation than they were qualified for, in order to fulfill responsibilities at home.

Downsizing Ambition

Given the tour of women's careers we've just taken, is it any surprise that women find it difficult to claim or sustain ambition? The survey shows that while almost half of the men consider themselves extremely or very ambitious, only about a third of the women do. (The proportion rises among women in business and the professions of law and medicine; there, 43% and 51%, respectively, consider themselves very ambitious.) In a similar vein, only 15% of highly qualified women (and 27% in the business sector) single out "a powerful position" as an important career goal; in fact, this goal ranked lowest in women's priorities in every sector we surveyed.

Far more important to these women are other items on the workplace wish list: the ability to associate with people they respect (82%); the freedom to "be themselves" at work (79%); and the opportunity to be flexible with their schedules (64%). Fully 61% of women consider it extremely or very important to have the opportunity to collaborate with others and work as part of a team. A majority (56%) believe it is very important for them to be able to give back to the community through their work. And 51% find "recognition from my company" either extremely or very important.

These top priorities constitute a departure from the traditional male take on ambition. Moreover, further analysis points to a disturbing age gap. In the business sector, 53% of younger women (ages 28 to 40) own up to being very ambitious, as contrasted with only 37% of older women. This makes sense in light of Anna Fels's groundbreaking work on women and ambition. In a 2004 HBR article, Fels argues convincingly that ambition stands on two legs— mastery and recognition. To hold onto their dreams, not only must women attain the necessary skills and experience, they must also have their achievements appropriately recognized. To the extent the latter is missing in female careers, ambition is undermined. A vicious cycle emerges: As women's ambitions stall, they are perceived as less committed, they no longer get the best assignments, and this lowers their ambitions further.

In our focus groups, we heard the disappointment—and discouragement—of women who had reached senior levels in corporations only to find the glass ceiling still in place, despite years of diversity initiatives. These women feel that they are languishing and have not been given either the opportunities or the recognition that would allow them to realize their full potential. Many feel handicapped in the attainment of their goals. The result is the vicious cycle that Fels describes: a "downsizing" of women's ambition that becomes a self-fulfilling prophecy. And the discrepancy in ambition levels between men and women has an insidious side effect in that it results in insufficient role models for younger women.

Reversing the Brain Drain

These, then, are the hard facts. With them in hand, we move from anecdotes to data—and, more important, to a different, richer analytical understanding of the problem. In the structural issue of off-ramps and on-ramps, we see the mechanism derailing the careers of highly qualified women and also the focal point for making positive change. What are the implications for corporate America? One thing at least seems clear: Employers can no longer pretend that treating women as "men in skirts" will fix their retention problems. Like it or not, large numbers of highly qualified, committed women need to take time out. The trick is to help them maintain connections that will allow them to come back from that time without being marginalized for the rest of their careers.

Create reduced-hour jobs

The most obvious way to stay connected is to offer women with demanding lives a way to keep a hand in their chosen field, short of full-time involvement. Our survey found that, in business sectors, fully 89% of women believe that access to reduced-hour jobs is important. Across all sectors, the figure is 82%.

The Johnson & Johnson family of companies has seen the increased loyalty and productivity that can result from such arrangements. We recently held a focus group with 12 part-time managers

How Ernst & Young Keeps Women on the Path to Partnership

IN THE MID-1990S, turnover among female employees at Ernst & Young was much higher than it was among male peers. Company leaders knew something was seriously wrong; for many years, its entering classes of young auditors had been made up of nearly equal numbers of men and women—yet it was still the case that only a tiny percentage of its partnership was female. This was a major problem. Turnover in client-serving roles meant lost continuity on work assignments. And on top of losing talent that the firm had invested in training, E&Y was incurring costs averaging 150% of a departing employee's annual salary just to fill the vacant position.

E&Y set a new course, marked by several important features outlined here. Since E&Y began this work, the percentage of women partners has more than tripled to 12% and the downward trend in retention of women at every level has been reversed. E&Y now has four women on the management board, and many more women are in key operating and client serving roles. Among its women partners, 10% work on a flexible schedule and more than 20 have been promoted to partner while working a reduced schedule. In 2004, 22% of new partners were women.

Focus

Regional pilot projects targeted five areas for improvement: Palo Alto and San Jose focused on life balance, Minneapolis on mentoring, New Jersey on flexible work arrangements, Boston on women networking in the business community, and Washington, DC, on women networking inside E&Y. Successful solutions were rolled out across the firm.

Committed Leadership

Philip Laskawy, E&Y's chairman from 1994 to 2001, made it a priority to retain and promote women. He convened a diversity task force of partners to focus on the problem and created an Office of Retention. Laskawy's successor, Jim Turley, deepened the focus on diversity by rolling out a People First strategy.

Policies

Ernst & Young equipped all its people for telework and made it policy that flexible work schedules would not affect anyone's opportunity for advancement. The new premise was that all jobs could be done flexibly.

New Roles

E&Y's Center for the New Workforce dedicates its staff of seven to developing and advancing women into leadership roles. A strategy team of three professionals addresses the firm's flexibility goals for both men and women. Also, certain partners are designated as "career watchers" and track individual women's progress, in particular, monitoring the caliber of the projects and clients to which they are assigned.

Learning Resources

All employees can use E&Y's Achieving Flexibility Web site to learn about flexible work arrangements. They can track how certain FWAs were negotiated and structured and can use the contact information provided in the database to ask those employees questions about how it is (or isn't) working.

Peer Networking

Professional Women's Networks are active in 41 offices, and they focus on building the skills, confidence, leadership opportunities, and networks necessary for women to be successful. A three-day Women's Leadership Conference is held every 18 months. The most recent was attended by more than 425 women partners, principals, and directors.

Accountability

The annual People Point survey allows employees to rate managers on how well they foster an inclusive, flexible work environment. Managers are also evaluated on metrics like number of women serving key accounts, in key leadership jobs, and in the partner pipeline.

at these companies and found a level of commitment that was palpable. The women had logged histories with J&J that ranged from eight to 19 years and spoke of the corporation with great affection. All had a focus on productivity and pushed themselves to deliver at the same level they had achieved before switching to part-time. One woman, a 15-year J&J veteran, was particularly eloquent in her gratitude to the corporation. She had had her first child at age 40 and, like so many new mothers, felt torn apart by the conflicting demands of home and work. In her words, "I thought I only had two choices—work full-time or leave—and I didn't want either. J&J's reduced-hour option has been a savior." All the women in the room were clear on one point: They would have quit had part-time jobs not been available.

At Pfizer, the deal is sweetened further for part-time workers; field sales professionals in the company's Vista Rx division are given access to the same benefits and training as full-time employees but work 60% of the hours (with a corresponding difference in base pay). Many opt for a three-day workweek; others structure their working day around children's school hours. These 230 employees—93% of whom are working mothers—remain eligible for promotion and may return to full-time status at their discretion.

Provide flexibility in the day

Some women don't require reduced work hours; they merely need flexibility in when, where, and how they do their work. Even parents who employ nannies or have children in day care, for example, must make time for teacher conferences, medical appointments, volunteering, child-related errands—not to mention the days the nanny calls in sick or the day care center is closed. Someone caring for an invalid or a fragile elderly person may likewise have many hours of potentially productive time in a day yet not be able to stray far from home.

For these and other reasons, almost two-thirds (64%) of the women we surveyed cite flexible work arrangements as being either extremely or very important to them. In fact, by a considerable margin, highly qualified women find flexibility more important than compensation; only 42% say that "earning a lot of money" is an important motivator. In our focus groups, we heard women use terms like "nirvana" and "the golden ring" to describe employment arrangements that allow them to flex their workdays, their work-weeks, and their careers. A senior employee who recently joined Lehman Brothers' equity division is an example. She had been working at another financial services company when a Lehman recruiter called. "The person who had been in the job previously was working one day a week from home, so they offered that opportunity to me. Though I was content in my current job," she told us, "that intriguing possibility made me reevaluate. In the end, I took the job at Lehman. Working from home one day a week was a huge lure."

Provide flexibility in the arc of a career

Booz Allen Hamilton, the management and technology consulting firm, recognized that it isn't simply a workday, or a workweek, that needs to be made more flexible. It's the entire arc of a career.

Management consulting as a profession loses twice as many women as men in the middle reaches of career ladders. A big part of the problem is that, perhaps more than in any other business sector, it is driven by an up-or-out ethos; client-serving professionals must progress steadily or fall by the wayside. The strongest contenders make partner through a relentless winnowing process. While many firms take care to make the separations as painless as possible (the chaff, after all, tends to land in organizations that might employ their services), there are clear limits to their patience. Typically, if a valued professional is unable to keep pace with the road warrior lifestyle, the best she can hope for is reassignment to a staff job.

Over the past year, Booz Allen has initiated a "ramp up, ramp down" flexible program to allow professionals to balance work and life and still do the client work they find most interesting. The key to the program is Booz Allen's effort to "unbundle" standard consult-ing projects and identify chunks that can be done by telecommuting or shorts stints in the office. Participating professionals are either regular employees or alumni that sign standard employment con-tracts and are activated as needed. For the professional, it's a way to take on a manageable amount of the kind of work they do best. For Booz Allen, it's a way to maintain ties to consultants who have already proved their merit in a challenging profession. Since many of these talented women will eventually return to full-time consulting employment, Booz Allen wants to be their employer of choice—and to keep their skills sharp in the meantime.

When asked how the program is being received, DeAnne Aguirre, a vice president at Booz Allen who was involved in its design (and who is also a member of our task force), had an instant reaction: "I think it's instilled new hope—a lot of young women I work with no longer feel that they will have to sacrifice some precious part of themselves." Aguirre explains that trade-offs are inevitable, but at Booz Allen an off-ramping decision doesn't have to be a devastating one anymore. "Flex careers are bound to be slower than conventional ones, but in ten years' time you probably won't remember the precise year you made partner. The point here is to remain on track and vitally connected."

Remove the stigma

Making flexible arrangements succeed over the long term is hard work. It means crafting an imaginative set of policies, but even more important, it means eliminating the stigma that is often attached to such nonstandard work arrangements. As many as 35% of the women we surveyed report various aspects of their organizations' cultures that effectively penalize people who take advantage of work-life policies. Telecommuting appears to be most stigmatized, with 39% of women reporting some form of tacit resistance to it, followed by job sharing and part-time work. Of flexible work arrangements in general, 21% report that "there is an unspoken rule at my workplace that people who use these options will not be promoted." Parental leave policies get more respect—though even here, 19% of women report cultural or attitudinal barriers to taking the time off that they are entitled to. In environments where flexible work arrangements are tacitly deemed illegitimate, many women would rather resign than request them.

Interestingly, when it comes to taking advantage of work-life policies, men encounter even more stigma. For example, 48% of the men we surveyed perceived job sharing as illegitimate in their workplace culture—even when it's part of official policy.

Transformation of the corporate culture seems to be a prerequisite for success on the work-life front. Those people at or near the top of an organization need to have that "eureka" moment, when they not only understand the business imperative for imaginative work-life policies but are prepared to embrace them, and in so doing remove the stigma. In the words of Dessa Bokides, treasurer at Pitney Bowes, "Only a leader's devotion to these issues will give others permission to transform conventional career paths."

Stop burning bridges

One particularly dramatic finding of our survey deserves special mention: Only 5% of highly qualified women looking for on-ramps are interested in rejoining the companies they left. In business sectors, that percentage is zero. If ever there was a danger signal for corporations, this is it.

The finding implies that the vast majority of off-ramped women, at the moment they left their careers, felt ill-used—or at least underutilized and unappreciated—by their employers. We can only speculate as to why this was. In some cases, perhaps, the situation ended badly; a woman, attempting impossible juggling feats, started dropping balls. Or an employer, embittered by the loss of too many "star" women, lets this one go much too easily.

It's understandable for managers to assume that women leave mainly for "pull" reasons and that there's no point in trying to keep them. Indeed, when family overload and the traditional division of labor place unmanageable demands on a working woman, it does appear that quitting has much more to do with what's going on at home than what's going on at work. However, it is important to realize that even when pull factors seem to be dominant, push factors are also in play. Most off-ramping decisions are conditioned by policies, practices, and attitudes at work. Recognition, flexibility, and the opportunity to telecommute—especially when endorsed by the corporate culture—can make a huge difference.

The point is, managers will not stay in a departing employee's good graces unless they take the time to explore the reasons for off-ramping and are able and willing to offer options short of total severance. If a company wants future access to this talent, it will need to go beyond the perfunctory exit interview and, at the very least, impart the message that the door is open. Better still, it will maintain a connection with off-ramped employees through a formal alumni program.

Provide outlets for altruism

Imaginative attachment policies notwithstanding, some women have no interest in returning to their old organizations because their desire to work in their former field has waned. Recall the focus group participants who spoke of a deepened desire to give back to the community after taking a hiatus from work. Remember, too, that women in business sectors are pushed off track more by dissatisfaction with work than pulled by external demands. Our data suggest that fully 52% of women with MBAs in the business sector cite the fact that they do not find their careers "either satisfying or enjoyable" as an important reason for why they left work. Perhaps not surprisingly, then, a majority (54%) of the women looking for on-ramps want to change their profession or field. And in most of those cases, it's a woman who formerly worked in the corporate sphere hoping to move into the not-for-profit sector.

Employers would be well advised to recognize and harness the altruism of these women. Supporting female professionals in their advocacy and public service efforts serves to win their energy and loyalty. Companies may also be able to redirect women's desire to give back to the community by asking them to become involved in mentoring and formal women's networks within the company.

Nurture ambition

Finally, if women are to sustain their passion for work and their competitive edge—whether or not they take formal time out—they must keep ambition alive. Our findings point to an urgent need to implement mentoring and networking programs that help women expand and sustain their professional aspirations. Companies like American Express, GE, Goldman Sachs, Johnson & Johnson, Lehman Brothers, and Time Warner are developing "old girls networks" that build skills, contacts, and confidence. They link women to inside power brokers and to outside business players and effectively inculcate those precious rainmaking skills.

Networks (with fund-raising and friend-raising functions) can enhance client connections. But they also play another, critical role. They provide the infrastructure within which women can earn recognition, as well as a safe platform from which to blow one's own horn without being perceived as too pushy. In the words of Patricia Fili-Krushel, executive vice president of Time Warner, "Company-sponsored women's networks encourage women to cultivate both sides of the power equation. Women hone their own leadership abilities but also learn to use power on behalf of others. Both skill sets help us increase our pipeline of talented women."

Adopt an On-Ramp

As we write this, market and economic factors, both cyclical and structural, are aligned in ways guaranteed to make talent constraints and skill shortages huge issues again. Unemployment is down and labor markets are beginning to tighten, just as the baby-bust generation is about to hit "prime time" and the number of workers between the ages of 35 to 45 is shrinking. Immigration levels are stable, so there's little chance of relief there. Likewise, productivity improvements are flattening. The phenomenon that bailed us out of our last big labor crunch—the entry for the first time of millions of women into the labor force—is not available to us again. Add it all up, and CEOs are back to wondering how they will find enough high-caliber talent to drive growth.

There is a winning strategy. It revolves around the retention and reattachment of highly qualified women. America these days has a large and impressive pool of female talent. Fifty-eight percent of college graduates are now women, and nearly half of all professional and graduate degrees are earned by women. Even more important, the incremental additions to the talent pool will be disproportionately female, according to figures released by the U.S. Department of Education. The number of women with graduate and professional degrees is projected to grow by 16% over the next decade, while the number of men with these degrees is projected to grow by a mere 1.3%. Companies are beginning to pay attention to these figures. As Melinda Wolfe, head of global leadership and diversity at Goldman Sachs, recently pointed out, "A large part of the potential talent pool consists of females and historically underrepresented groups. With the professional labor market tightening, it is in our direct interest to give serious attention to these matters of retention and reattachment."

In short, the talent is there; the challenge is to create the circumstances that allow businesses to take advantage of it over the long run. To tap this all-important resource, companies must understand the complexities of women's nonlinear careers and be prepared to support rather than punish those who take alternate routes.

Originally published in March 2005. Reprint R0503B

Sheryl Sandberg

The HBR Interview. *An interview with Sheryl Sandberg by Adi Ignatius*

Shortly after publication of her blockbuster book Lean In: Women, Work, and the Will to Lead, *Facebook COO Sheryl Sandberg sat down to discuss gender issues in the workplace with HBR editor in chief Adi Ignatius. Here are excerpts from the conversation.*

Adi Ignatius: *Who is the book for? And what is the ultimate or primary takeaway you would like people to take from it?*

Sheryl Sandberg: I think the book is for any woman who wants advice on how to sit at any table she wants to sit at and any man who wants to be part of creating a more equal world, both at home and in the workforce.

We know that institutions that use the talents of the full workforce perform better. There's data that suggests that. I think that increasingly will be proven to be true. We also know that more-equal marriages are happier and more stable. So there's a lot of potential for this to have very positive effects for our organizations and for our homes.

You're doing a big publicity rollout—Oprah, Time *magazine, other things. You've become, effectively, a major spokesperson for some of these topics. How do you fit that into your world? How does that fit or conflict with what you're doing at Facebook?*

It's really complementary to my work at Facebook if I want us to build the best products. One of the ways we do that is to attract and retain the very best people. And that means attracting and retaining men *and* women.

Organizations will tell you exactly what the data shows. They get women in the door, but then, at the senior levels, they lose them. Warren Buffett has said, I think quite graciously and famously, that he only had to compete with half the population. If more people get in the race, the running time is going to be faster. We need to get more people in the race and get more people to stay in the race.

Back to the question of Facebook. If people pay attention to your message, you will have helped every company. You will have helped your competitors as well as Facebook. So how do you know when it's too much? How do you wall off what is becoming a bigger, and bigger, and bigger role for yourself?

I still spend a very small fraction of time on this, compared to the time I spend on Facebook. But I do think that it's a message that helps Facebook. Ever since I've been more public on women, we have a great track record at getting amazing women to apply and getting strong women to stay. This helps make the workplace better for men, too.

A couple of years ago, I had a morning meeting, and there was a man who worked here who missed the meeting. He sent me an email and said, "Hey, I missed your meeting. Just wanted you to know the reason I missed your meeting is, because of your encouragement, I take my kids to school half the time now. Thank you. And I knew I could miss your meeting"—and it was a big meeting—"because of that. Thank you. This is why I love working here."

He wasn't playing you?

I guess he could have been. Ask him. But he's still here, and he's really happy and he's a star. And when you ask him why he's here, he'll say, "I love Facebook's mission. I love what you're doing. And I love that you care about my life, too." And that is, I think, pretty unique, but it makes our employees pretty loyal.

I often try to interview female executives and CEOs, and I say, "I'd like to talk to you about the experience of being a female business leader in what is still essentially a boy's club." And usually the response I get—and you talk about it in the book—is, "Look, I don't view myself as 'a female CEO.' I'm just 'a CEO.'" And I wonder—I understand that for public consumption people have to say that, but surely there's a difference. What can be learned from female experience in roles like this?

All of us do that. I did that. Had you asked me that question five years ago, I would have said the same thing. And there's a reason we don't talk about gender. No one talks about gender in the workplace.

Women don't talk about it, because you're afraid if you say the words, "I'm a woman," basically what the other person is going to hear is, "I want special treatment" or "I'm going to sue you." Neither of which you mean, but that's what they hear.

And a man who runs a large organization told me—and won't go on record, so he means it—that it's easier to talk about your sex life in public than it is to talk about gender. One of the goals I have with writing *Lean In* is really to make gender an OK topic in the workplace, because there are so many things that would make this all work better if we would discuss it.

So is the idea then that men and women become more like each other? Or that we really celebrate the differences—not try to minimize them, but identify them and kind of celebrate them?

I think we want to understand the differences and celebrate them. We want to break down the stereotypical limitations to our choices.

See, I don't think we have a real choice. When people say the word "choice," what they mean is women can choose to work or stay home. They don't really mean that men can work in the home and be as respected as a woman can. Of all the working families with two parents and one parent is an at-home full-time parent, 4% of those are men—4%. We don't really have choice for men. Men are not encouraged. I have friends, male friends, who have tried to do that. Some of them still do. The world is not very welcoming, respectful, or encouraging of the idea that it's a great job to be a full-time at-home dad, and we need to change that. We need to stop naming the class "Mommy and Me." "Mommy and Me" is not welcoming to fathers.

And the same thing for women—we don't really encourage leadership for women. We try. But we know that we call our daughters "bossy" and not our sons. Women are given these messages that are not very subtle all through their lives that are really very antileadership.

What I'm hoping to be part of doing—and just play my own small part—is broadening those choices. Because if we broaden those choices, we end up in a world where all of us have more opportunity. And we should have better results as a result of that opportunity.

In your book, you anticipated some of the criticisms. You've mentioned some of the criticisms you faced in the past and anticipated some of them, then you rounded them. Anne-Marie Slaughter, in her piece in The Atlantic, *said, in a sense, the arguments that you're making are, on one level, blaming women—you know, "What is wrong with you?" Her argument is that that's sort of misplaced. That it's asking too much of women, and it's putting the blame where it doesn't belong. How do you respond to that argument?*

There are all kinds of hurdles women face. Women face huge numbers of institutional barriers, discrimination, assumptions about them, lack of flexibility—all of the things she talked about, which are absolutely real.

We also face barriers that exist within ourselves or that are the results of the socialization we've been given. We are told, really, women shouldn't have strong voices, women shouldn't sit at tables. And then we internalize that and we do it to ourselves. It takes both.

We have to break down the institutional barriers women face. One of the best ways to do that, and the fastest way, is to get more women into positions of power, so that they can do it. You know, Google has pregnancy parking because I got pregnant, and I was senior enough when I realized it was really hard to walk from the back of the parking lot all the way to the front. I was senior enough to walk into Larry Page and Sergey Brin's office and say, "We need pregnancy parking." And Sergey looked up and said, "We sure do. I never thought of it." I never thought of it either, but I was a senior-enough woman to demand it. And I'm long gone from Google, but pregnancy parking is still there. So one of the best ways to break down those institutional barriers is for women to get those positions of power. Men can also do it. But we also need to talk about the internal barriers we face.

I'm not trying to have the whole debate. I'm not trying to say it's the whole answer. I'm trying to add to this side of the debate, because I think it takes both. And that doesn't mean we're blaming women. It means we're helping them see what they have the power to do.

Alice Walker has this great quote I love—and I won't get it exactly right without looking it up—but the fastest way to give up power is to think you don't have any. There is so much we can do. So much we can do. And I think that's the most empowering part of when someone tells me there's a big problem. That's great, but if they tell me there's a big problem and I can be part of fixing it, that's so much more empowering.

You got a lot of attention for telling people that you go home at 5:30. Shouldn't we all go home at 5:30? And shouldn't we all go home at 5:30 and shut off?

We should all find ways to be able to do the things we want to do in our lives. And I'm not, in any of this—the book or going home at 5:30—trying to be prescriptive and say, "Here's what I do and everyone should do what I do."

When I said publicly, "I'm coming home at 5:30," I took a deep breath. I mean, that's a hard thing to admit, no matter where you are in your career. But I did it on purpose to say to people, "Look, this is how I'm doing this. I can be both a mother and a professional. And I do it by going home at 5:30."

I also said, "I go home at 5:30. My kids are young. I have dinner with them, put them in the bath, put them to bed, and then get back online." We want people to have the flexibility they need. And it's not just people with children; it's people without children.

When I was in business school there was a women-in-consulting panel. I was thinking about going into consulting, so I went. There were a couple of women on the panel, and they asked questions, you know, "How do you do it all?" And there was one single woman without kids.

She said, "I'm so tired of people telling everyone else with kids that they need to go home. It's as if going home for your kid's soccer game or your kids' dinner is so legitimate. I need to go to a bar. I need to go to a bar, so I can preserve the option to meet someone, so I can one day have a kid."

Workplace flexibility is important for all of us. And for me, it's going home at 5:30, but for you, it might be something else. But we need as much flexibility as we can give ourselves and each other.

One of the phrases you use in the book is about "reigniting the revolution." Talk a little bit about that. How would that revolution unfold?

I think what's happened is that women are making more and more progress at every level, except the leadership level. We got 50% of the college degrees 30 years ago. We are getting more and more college degrees every year, more and more graduate degrees, more and more entry-level jobs. But progress at the top has stalled.

Women have had 14% to 15% of the C-level jobs in corporate America for 10 years. We've had 16% to 17% of the board seats for 10 years. It's not moving anymore. We have to understand that if the revolution was so that women would have an equal voice in the decisions that are made in our world, it's stalled.

And decisions are made at every table. They're made in the boardroom, and they're made at the PTA meeting. There aren't enough women sitting at those tables, and there aren't enough women sitting at the tables where decisions are made.

So if I talk about "reigniting the revolution," what I mean is, one, I want us to notice. People watch my TED talk, and it starts out with the fact that women are not getting their share of the top jobs anywhere in the world. People find that shocking. They're shocked. "Really? I thought women were taking over!"

Well, if having 15% is "taking over" or 20% of Congress—look at the recent Congressional elections. There were all these headlines: "Women are taking over the Congress." Twenty percent is not taking over. Twenty percent is one-fifth. We have to recognize that we're going to have to do something differently if we want more seats at the table where decisions are made. And I would like more women to have more seats at those tables.

There are people who will read this book and will say, "OK, there's some interesting ideas here, but is Sheryl Sandberg a reasonable role model?" It's both criticism and praise. "She's top of her class at Harvard, she has a great job, and she doesn't understand the struggles that other women are facing every day." And at that point there's a disconnect.

I'm incredibly fortunate. I've had incredible opportunities, mentors, and support. And I'm really grateful for all of that. A lot of what this book is about and a lot of the struggles are the same struggles many women face. The struggle to believe in yourself. The struggle to not feel guilty. To get enough sleep. To believe that you can be both a professional and a parent.

Both anecdotally from all the comments and letters that I got after the TED talk, and in all the research and data, these are very common themes across women. This isn't about me, and I don't hold myself out as the role model everyone should follow. I am trying to be honest about the choices I face. I'm trying to give voice to the struggles we don't talk about that women face in the workplace, so that all women and men can be part of moving toward an equal world.

Can you talk about some concrete things that Facebook or other companies are doing?

A whole bunch of things. Organizations holding people responsible for *results*, not the *appearance* of trying to get results. There is a culture of face time. It's so prevalent that people want to hold themselves responsible for results.

We had an employee here for a while who, really famously, didn't come in very much. But he absolutely did an unbelievable job for this company. And we would all joke about it all the time. Like, "Nice of you to come to the office."

We had an employee here for a while, who really, no one had ever met. Literally, no one had met this guy. He coded at his house. He really didn't like talking to people. But he built the most amazing products. And he became really well known, so no one cared if they ever saw him.

Now, not every organization can have the flexibility of Silicon Valley, certainly not retail, but almost all organizations can have more flexibility, and it starts with holding people accountable for results, not the appearance of having results.

Talking about gender, how are we going to get women to take the steps they need to take to come back after maternity leave if we will never say to them, "What are your plans?" How do we talk about women, tell them not to lean back—I call it, "Don't leave before you leave"—how do we talk to women about not leaving before they leave if we're never willing to talk about it?

Just talking about gender—Ken Chenault [who served as chairman and CEO of American Express from 2001–2018] is an amazing example. The data shows very clearly that women get interrupted more than men. If that happens in a meeting Ken is at—and I've heard this from Ken and from others at American Express—he stops the meeting and says, "You know, you just interrupted her." That completely changes behavior. Think about the business results of that. He's now going to run a company where you get the best results from everyone, because everyone's voice is heard at the table.

Formal programs for mentorship and sponsorship—or, I don't know if it has to be formal or informal—but explicitly encouraging men to sponsor women . . . the data shows really clearly that the majority of men in the workplace are afraid to be alone with a woman. That is such a big deal. Mentorship is all about being alone with a person and talking to them one-on-one. Mentorship is all about that. So if the majority of men in the workplace are afraid to be alone with a woman, how are we going to get men to mentor women? And if the majority of the people in positions of power are men, how do we get men to mentor and sponsor women?

Acknowledging and explicitly encouraging men and women at the senior levels to mentor women not only gives men permission, it says that it should be a badge of honor to be alone with a woman talking about her career. You shouldn't see someone walking by and be nervous that someone is going to see you. You should be proud that you're having those conversations. Organizations need to do that.

You obviously had a fabulous mentor in Larry Summers. I don't think I've ever had a mentor. To what extent did that help you? How does somebody find a mentor like that?

I think it helped tremendously. I've had a lot of mentors over the course of my career, Larry being one of the absolutely most important and certainly the first. But you know, Larry offered to be my thesis adviser in college, and then he took me with him to the World Bank. Then he offered me a job at the Treasury. Those opportunities are ones I wouldn't have had without him.

There's two different messages. The message for people in power, both men and women, is to mentor—and mentor women, not just men. We tend to mentor and hire people like us. We don't mean to do it. Women do it, too. But that means that more men get mentored. And that is the perpetuation of the boys' network that I don't think anyone wants, even the men who are doing it, probably inadvertently. We need to be telling them, explicitly, to mentor women.

For women, I think, we are in a very dangerous place, where we keep telling women how important it is to get mentors and sponsors. So then women walk up to strangers and say, "Will you be my mentor? Will you be my sponsor?" and that's not how it works. That's not how a relationship is formed. You have to find real ways to build a relationship, and getting the right message to the right group is super important.

You talk a lot about likability. I want to ask a couple questions about that. First, and maybe data bears this out, that there's this assumption that we, that society, that people generally don't like female leaders. Why is that the default? Why don't we love female leaders?

This is really important, and I think, the heart. And this is what I did not understand when I was in business school. I didn't understand until a few years ago. Even though I kind of knew it, I felt it intuitively, but I didn't understand the data. What the data shows more strongly than anything else in the differences about men and women is that success and likability are positively correlated for men and negatively correlated for women, which means that as someone gets more successful, they are liked less. Both men and women like them less if they're a woman, and both men women like them more if they're a man.

Decades of social science research say that we want people to conform to our stereotypical views. We do. And when they don't conform to our stereotypical views, we don't like them as much. So we expect men to have some leadership qualities, to be providers, to be aggressive, to have opinions, to speak out. We expect women to have communal qualities, to be givers and sharers and working for the common good, not for themselves. And we hold people to those stereotypes.

So when a man says, "Here's my opinion, and here's why you should do it" or "Here's why I deserve a raise," he is conforming to our stereotype, and it's all good. When a woman says, "Here's what we should do" or "Here's why I want a raise," rather than "Here's what *the team* should do" or "Here's what I want for *you*," she's going against our stereotypical views, and we don't like her.

The problem is that we want to promote and hire people who are both competent and liked. And that's just so much easier for men than women. I think there's a short-term answer and a long-term answer. The short-term answers are that we have to talk about this honestly, because actually talking about this changes the dynamic. If you tell people that everyone has a fine reaction to a man asking for a raise but a negative reaction to a woman, once you tell someone that, their reaction the next time a woman asks for a raise changes. Simply putting sunlight on that—explaining it—changes it.

The second is, we have to be realists. There's some great work going on at HBS and Harvard on how women have to negotiate differently. When I was negotiating with Mark Zuckerberg, I didn't just get to say, "Here's what I want to be paid." I only did this implicitly; I hadn't done the research. But I said, "You're hiring me to lead your negotiating teams. You want me to be a good negotiator. I'm bringing those same skills." And then I negotiated, and I think it went better, so we need to teach women what to do.

But the real solution—which is probably not as immediate but is hopefully medium-term, not even long-term—is that if we just got more women in leadership roles and more men in nurturing roles, our fundamental assumptions would change. It would no longer violate our assumptions of what a woman is to see her as a leader. It wouldn't be so unusual. And then that negative reaction we're all having would go away.

At a certain level, I read your book and thought, Wow, finding a great husband—I don't know how many potentials there are out there—is as good a determinant as any, for—

It's the most important career decision a woman makes. Single. The *single* most important career decision a woman makes is if she's going to have a life partner and if that partner is going to support her career. And "support that career" does not mean, "Oh, honey, I support you." Supporting her career means getting up in the middle of the night and changing half the diapers. Number one determinant.

I feel like, anecdotally, men are getting better in that respect. Is there any data that says that?

Oh, they're getting way better. But they're still doing much, much, much less than half. So in a married couple, both of whom work full-time, the woman will do 30% more child care and 40% more housework than a man—much better than the previous generation, but women still largely have two jobs and men have one. If men will do more of the work at home to support them—and you know, the stereotype of a successful professional woman has long been that she wasn't married. But that's not true. Most of the successful professional women *are* married, which means they have partners, and those women have successful partners. I don't know any successful woman who, if she has a partner—and some don't, but if she does—whose partner is not super supportive.

I think I'm right in quoting you as having said at one point, that at your age—and you're not even remotely old, 43—that it's too late for your generation. I didn't quite understand that.

I don't believe that women in my generation will achieve 50% of the top jobs in any industry. But I hope to still be alive when we get to 50% of Congress or we get to 50% of the CEO jobs. But I don't believe it will be my peers who do that. I would love to be wrong.

So it's not too late to join the struggle or to push the ideas.

Absolutely. It's not too late. And we can keep increasing, but with no progress in these 10, 15 years—the numbers are going to have to be very, very dramatic for that to happen. We need to commit ourselves to those working toward it happening.

If my book is a "manifesto" or "feminist manifesto," it's one that is saying we need to commit to real equality. And what real equality means is more women in leadership roles and more men helping in the home.

You're a Harvard Business School grad. This is HBS's 50th anniversary of accepting women there. What should HBS be doing differently? What should institutions like that be doing before you get to the professional level?

HBS is an example in my book of one of the institutions that's actually done the best job. Frances Frei and Youngme Moon are models that everyone should be following. And Dean Nitin Nohria is a hero of this.

Forever at HBS, American men have outperformed international students and women. A couple of years ago, Frances Frei and Youngme Moon came in and said, "We're going to broaden our definition of leadership." They gave a broader definition of leadership, holding people responsible not just for their own behavior but for making other people better. And they worked on the soft stuff. They held everyone accountable, and then they worked on some curriculum things (but they were actually pretty small).

They had a field study, and if you look, in two years they closed the educational achievement gap at Harvard. In two years. An achievement gap that was there when I was there. What's so exciting is that the satisfaction of the students went up, including the American men. And that, I think, is such an important example.

They started talking about gender. They walked around and told people: "There's an academic gap between our male American students and women and international students." They started talking about why. They broadened the definition of leadership. I mean, this is not that hard to do, but they made it explicit and they did it in two years. Harvard Business School is a very established institution. I think it's such a great example for what other organizations can do. But we have to talk about gender to do it. This will not happen without talking about gender.

I think the biggest challenge you're going to have—and these ideas are going to have—is simply a sense that people have been fighting this battle for decades. And your book points out how small the progress has been.

Yeah. But I think now is our time. I really believe this, that now is the time. That the external barriers, which are still there, are just so much lower than they were. And, you know, my mother was told by her parents, school, professors, and everyone that she could be a nurse or a teacher. That's what they told her. "You have two choices. You can be a nurse or a teacher." That is not where we are.

My childhood was the childhood of firsts. The first woman in space, the first woman Speaker of the House. This is within our grasp, and HBS shows that these cultural shifts can happen. If we start acknowledging what the real issues are, we can solve them. And it's not that hard if we're committed to doing it.

Originally published as an HBR IdeaCast, March 14, 2013.

About the Contributors

LINDA L. CARLI is an associate professor of psychology at Wellesley College, in Massachusetts; her current research focus is on gender discrimination and other challenges faced by professional women. She is the coauthor (with Alice H. Eagly) of *Through the Labyrinth: The Truth About How Women Become Leaders* (Harvard Business School Press, 2007).

FRANK DOBBIN is a professor of sociology at Harvard University.

ALICE H. EAGLY is the James Padilla Chair of Arts and Sciences and a professor of psychology at Northwestern University. She is the coauthor (with Linda L. Carli) of *Through the Labyrinth: The Truth About How Women Become Leaders* (Harvard Business School Press, 2007).

ROBIN ELY is the Diane Doerge Wilson Professor of Business Administration at Harvard Business School and the faculty chair of the HBS Gender Initiative.

ANNA FELS is a psychiatrist and a faculty member at Cornell University's Weill Medical College in New York. She is the author of *Necessary Dreams: Ambition in Women's Changing Lives*.

ALTON B. HARRIS is a law partner at Nixon Peabody. He has worked to promote gender equality in the workplace for more than 30 years. He is the coauthor (with Andrea S. Kramer) of *Breaking Through Bias: Communication Techniques for Women to Succeed at Work*. Learn more at andieandal.com or on Twitter @AndieandAl.

SYLVIA ANN HEWLETT is founder and CEO of the Center for Talent Innovation and author of *Forget a Mentor, Find a Sponsor* (Harvard Business Review Press, 2013).

HERMINIA IBARRA is the Charles Handy Chair and Professor of Organizational Behavior at London Business School. Prior to joining LBS, she served on the INSEAD and Harvard Business School faculties. An authority on leadership and career development, Ibarra is ranked among the most influential management thinkers in the world by Thinkers50. Her most recent book, *Act Like a Leader, Think Like a Leader* (Harvard Business Review Press, 2015), explains how to step up to a bigger leadership role. She received her PhD from Yale University, where she was a National Science Fellow.

ADI IGNATIUS is the editor in chief of *Harvard Business Review*.

ALEXANDRA KALEV is an associate professor of sociology at Tel Aviv University.

DEBORAH KOLB is the Deloitte Ellen Gabriel Professor for Women in Leadership (Emerita) and a cofounder of the Center for Gender in Organizations at Simmons College School of Management. An expert on negotiation and leadership, she is codirector of the Negotiations in the Workplace Project at the Program on Negotiation at Harvard Law School. She is the coauthor of *Negotiating at Work: Turn Small Wins into Big Gains*.

ANDREA S. KRAMER is a law partner at McDermott Will & Emery. She has worked to promote gender equality in the workplace for more than 30 years. She is the coauthor (with Alton B. Harris) of *Breaking Through Bias: Communication Techniques for Women to Succeed at Work*. Learn more at andieandal.com or on Twitter @AndieandAl.

SUZANNE LEBSOCK is the Emeritus Board of Governors Professor of History at Rutgers University, where she cofounded the top-ranked graduate program in the history of women and gender.

CAROLYN BUCK LUCE is executive in residence at the Center for Talent Innovation and senior managing director at Hewlett Consulting Partners. She is an adjunct professor at Columbia's Graduate School of International and Public Affairs and was previously the Global Pharmaceutical Sector Leader at Ernst & Young LLP.

HEATHER MCLAUGHLIN is an assistant professor at Oklahoma State University.

OTILIA OBODARU is a PhD student in organizational behavior at INSEAD.

RIPA RASHID specializes in global talent strategies. She has spent over a decade as a management consultant and has held senior positions at MetLife and Time Warner. She is coauthor with Sylvia Ann Hewlett of *Winning the War for Talent in Emerging Markets* (Harvard Business Review Press, 2011). She is a graduate of Harvard University and INSEAD's MBA program.

KATHLEEN REARDON is Professor Emerita at the University of Southern California Marshall School of Business and an expert in workplace politics, persuasion, and negotiation. She is the author of Amazon bestsellers *The Secret Handshake*, *It's All Politics*, and *Comebacks at Work*. Her blog and art website is www.kathleenkelleyreardon.com.

SHERYL SANDBERG is COO of Facebook and author of *Lean In: Women, Work, and the Will to Lead*, and coauthor, with Adam Grant, of *Option B: Facing Adversity, Building Resilience, and Finding Joy*.

DEBORAH TANNEN is University Professor and Professor of Linguistics at Georgetown University in Washington, D.C. She is the author of 12 books, including *You Just Don't Understand: Women and Men in Conversation*, which introduced to the general public the idea of female and male styles of communication, and *Talking from 9 to 5*, on which her *Harvard Business Review* article is based. Her most recent book is *You're the Only One I Can Tell: Inside the Language of Women's Friendships*.

JOAN C. WILLIAMS is a Distinguished Professor of Law and the founding director of the Center for WorkLife Law at the University of California Hastings College of the Law. She is a leading expert on social inequality. Her newest book is *White Working Class: Overcoming Class Cluelessness in America* (Harvard Business Review Press, 2017).

Index

accountability, 171
  See also social accountability
advertising, for open positions,
  16–17
agentic qualities, 8
Allen, Woody, 119–120
altruism, 176
alumni programs, 5, 19, 161
ambition
  aspects of, 22–25
  barriers to, 29–35, 168–169
  career goals and, 31–35
  childhood, 21–25
  cultural barriers and, 155
  downsizing, 168–169
  in emerging markets, 147
  fear of expressing, 25–29
  lack of female, 21–37
  mastery and, 23–25, 34, 37
  nurturing, 161, 176–177
  recognition and, 24–25, 168
  recommendations for, 32–33
  stress and, 36–37
antidiscrimination legislation, 16
apologies, 71, 78–79
assertive behavior, 9, 45
attention, deflecting, 25–29
authenticity, 10, 42
authority
  apologizing and, 79
  negotiating, 82–89
autonomy, 104

Bandura, Albert, 24
Barnes, Brenda, 157
barriers. *See* career barriers
Bem Sex Role Inventory (BSRI), 29–30
bias
  See also discrimination
  contact between groups to
    reduce, 111–113
  diversity training and, 104–109

  in emerging markets, 145–155
  gender, 7, 16, 39–40, 42–46, 50,
    150
  grievance procedures and, 108–109
  hiring tests and, 106–107, 116
  in performance ratings, 107–108
  social accountability and, 113–115
  tools for reducing, 109–118
boards of directors, women on, 1
boasting, 75–76
Boehringer Ingelheim, 154
Booz Allen Hamilton, 160, 173–174
Brazil, 145–146, 150, 151
Bush, George H. W., 58
business owners, female, 99

Campbell, Kim (former Canadian
    prime minister), 8
career barriers
  cultural, 155
  facing women, 2–15, 20, 29–35,
    39–50, 169, 182–183
career goals, 31–35
career paths
  flexible, 160–161, 173–174
  gendered, 44–45
  nonlinear, 166–167
  up or out, 18–19
  women leaving, 157–162
Carli, Linda L., 1–20
Carlson, Gretchen, 122
Chenault, Ken, 186
Cheng, Marietta Nien-hwa, 10
chief executive officers (CEOs),
    women as, 1
child care, 14, 32, 148
  See also family demands
childhood
  ambitions, 21–25
  linguistic styles learned in, 72–73
  play groups in, 72–73, 76
  socialization in, 76, 84, 89

China, 145, 148, 150, 153
Clinton, Hillary, 48, 62
Coca-Cola, 111
cognitive dissonance, 109–110
collaboration, 13, 61–62
college
    gender differences in recognition
      in, 26–27
    recruitment programs in, 110–113,
      116, 117
college graduates, 147, 152, 178
commitment, to work, 42, 148, 169,
    170
communal qualities, 8, 9
communication, 52, 55, 67–89
    authority and, 82–89
    conversational rituals and,
      77–82
    with employees, 131–132
    indirectness in, 84–88
    linguistic style and, 68–77
    self-confidence and, 67–68
competence, 49, 63–64, 76
compliments, 80–81
confidence, 67–68, 70, 75–76
Conroy, Frank (author), 23–24
conversations
    rituals in, 77–82
    styles, 68–74, 88–89
    turn taking in, 69–70
corporate culture. See organiza-
    tional culture
Cox, Vivienne, 61–62
credibility, 42, 126–127
credit sharing, 70
credit taking, 74–75
crime, 151
criticism, giving, 83–84
cross-training, 112–113, 117
cultural attitudes
    in emerging markets, 145–146,
      148–151, 155

toward sexual harassment,
    119–130
toward women, 2
cultural barriers, 155
culture of exclusion, 101

decision making, 13, 67
developmental job experiences, 5,
    18, 46
developmental theory, 23
Dinesen, Isak, 37
discrimination
    See also bias; sexual harassment
    in emerging markets, 145–155
    gender, 7, 16, 36, 39–46, 50, 150
    grievance procedures, 108–109
    lawsuits, 103
    legislation against, 16
    in promotions, 6–7
    racial, 106, 111, 113–114
    wage, 5–6
    workplace, 34
diversity managers, 115, 117
diversity programs
    adverse effects of, 105–106
    bias and, 104–109
    engagement with, 109–111
    mandatory, 106, 116
    reasons for failure of, 103–118
    successful, 116–117
    tools for involving managers,
      109–118
    voluntary, 106, 116
diversity task forces, 114–115,
    117
Dobbin, Frank, 103–118
domestic responsibilities. See family
    demands
dominant behavior, in men and
    women, 9
double binds, 8–10, 13, 45, 47
drive theory of motivation, 23

Eagly, Alice H., 1–20
earnings
  See also wages
  patterns over life span, 166
  reduced, after time out of work-
    force, 164–167
education
  in emerging markets, 147, 152
  gender differences in recognition
    in, 26–27
  impact on wages, 6
  opportunities for, 35
  of women, 26–27, 35, 147, 152, 178
Eisenhower, Dwight D., 111–112
elder care, 145, 148–149, 159–160, 172
Ely, Robin, 39–50
emerging markets
  attracting and retaining talented
    women in, 151–155
  college graduates in, 147, 152
  commitment in, 148
  community ties in, 154–155
  family demands in, 148–149
  female talent in, 145–155
  gender bias in, 150
  levels of ambition in, 147–148
  networking in, 152–153
  public sector jobs in, 149
  research on talent in, 146–148
  travel and safety in, 150–151
emotional intelligence, 57
empathy, 28, 101
employment agencies, 16–17
engagement, 109–111
envisioning, 56
  See also vision/visioning
equal opportunities, 2, 35–36,
  88–89, 118
equality, progress toward gender, 11
Erikson, Erik, 23
Ernst & Young, 170–171
exclusion, culture of, 101

Facebook, 179–180, 185–187
family demands
  See also work/life balance
  in emerging markets, 145,
    148–149
  flexible work arrangements and,
    172–173
  lack of social capital and, 17–18
  off-ramping and, 157–162
  reduced-hour jobs and, 169, 172
  unequal distribution of, 13–14,
    160, 189–190
  on women, 4, 13–14, 32–33, 37,
    145, 148–149
  work hours and, 16
family-friendly HR practices, 5,
  18, 19
Farenthold, Blake, 123
Farrow, Ronan, 119–120
fathers
  stay-at-home, 181–182
  time spent on child care by, 14,
    189
feedback
  360-degree, 47, 51, 53, 59, 60
  giving, 56, 71, 79–80
Fels, Anna, 21–37
female brain drain, 157–178
  reversing, 169–177
feminine evil, 124
femininity, 29–35, 45, 49
feminism, 11
financial pressures, 162–163
financial services industry, 103
flexible work arrangements,
  160–161, 172–175, 183–184, 186
Fox, 126
Franken, Al, 120
Frei, Frances, 190–191
Frelinghuysen, Lisa Beattie, 158, 162
Freud, Sigmund, 23
Friedman, Ken, 127

gender bias, 7, 16, 39–46, 50, 150
   See also discrimination
gender differences, understanding
   and celebrating, 181–182
gendered work, 44–45
gender equality, progress toward, 11
gender gap
   interventions to diminish, 15–20
   lessening of, 11
   in promotions, 5, 6–7
   in wages, 5–6
General Electric (GE), 152–153
giving nature, 30
glass ceiling, 2–3, 20, 169
Global Executive Leadership Inventory (GELI), 56–57
global mindset, 57
Glovsky, Richard, 96–97
Goldberg, Philip, 7
Goldberg paradigm, 7
Google India Women in Engineering
   Award, 151–152
Greene, Lauren, 123
grievance procedures, 108–109, 117

Hackett, Isa, 128
Harris, Alton B., 130–137
Harvard Business School, 190–191
Hawken, Paul, 101
Hewlett, Sylvia Ann, 145–155,
   157–178
Hill, Anita, 121, 124
hiring tests, 106–107, 116
hostile work culture, 91–102,
   120–123, 134–137
housework, 13–14
Hughes, Karen, 157

Ibarra, Herminia, 39–50, 51–66
identity workspaces, 42, 46–48
Ignatius, Adi, 179–191
income sources, 162–163
India, 145, 148, 150, 151, 155

indirectness, 71, 84–88
informal networks, 45
institutional barriers, 182–183
international exposure, 154
investment banks, 103, 107

Jackman, Jay M., 98–100
job assignments
   developmental, 5, 18, 46
   overseas, 154
job interviews, 107
Johnson & Johnson, 169, 172
Judd, Ashley, 122

Kagan, Jerome, 24–25
Kalev, Alexandra, 103–118
Kolb, Deborah, 39–50
Kozinski, Alex, 123, 127
Kramer, Andrea S., 130–137
Krzyzewski, Mike, 10–11

laisse-faire leadership style, 12
language
   See also communication
   as social behavior, 70–74
   social dynamics of, 74
leadership style
   gender differences in, 59–61,
      64–66
   of women, 3, 4, 10–13
leaders/leadership
   components of, 56–57
   critical mass of female, 17
   development of, 40–42
   experience of female, 181
   future positions in, 11
   identity, 39–42, 66
   interventions to increase female,
      4–5, 15–20
   lack of women in top, 1–3,
      184–185
   laisse-faire, 12

likeability of, 187–189
vs. management, 58
masculinity and, 45
participative, 13
preparation for, 18
purpose, 41–42, 48–50
ratings of male and female,
    44–47, 55–57, 59, 65
resistance to women's, 4, 7–10
supporting women's access to,
    42–50
training programs, 5, 39, 40
transactional, 12
transformational, 12
transition to, 65–66
vision and, 51–66
*Lean In: Women, Work, and the Will
    to Lead* (Sandberg), 179–191
learning cycle, in recognition, 24
Lebsock, Suzanne, 119–130
Lehman Brothers, 173
Levine, James, 123
likability, 47, 49, 187–189
line management, preparation for,
    18
linguistic styles, 68–89
    about, 68–74
    conversational rituals and, 77–82
    differences in, 88–89
    indirectness, 84–88
    negotiating authority and, 82–89
    social dynamics and, 74–77
Luce, Carolyn Buck, 157–178

male networks, 15
management
    diversity programs and, 109–118
    interventions, to increase female
        leadership, 4–5, 15–20
    vs. leadership, 58
    racial makeup of, 103, 106, 107,
        109
    women in, 103–104, 106, 107, 109

managing up/down, 71, 83–84
Marineau, Philip A., 97–98
marriage, impact on wages, 6
masculinity, 30–32, 45
    toxic, 127
mastery, 23–25, 34, 37
maternity leave, 165, 186
McConnell, Mitch, 123
McLaughlin, Heather, 137–144
Mead, Margaret, 37
meetings
    communication styles in, 88–89
    contributions during, 73–74
men
    ambition of, 168
    domestic responsibilities and,
        13–14, 160, 189–190
    as full-time parents, 181–182
    leaving workforce, 162
    linguistic style of, 72–74
    participation of, in family-
        friendly benefits, 19, 175
    promotions for, 6–7
    qualities associated with, 8–10
    sexual harassment and, 119–120,
        122–123, 127
mentoring programs, 18, 39, 40,
    110–111, 113, 116, 177, 186–187
Merrill Lynch, 103
#MeToo movement, 92, 120–122,
    125, 137
Milano, Alyssa, 125
minorities
    bias against, 104–109, 118
    college recruitment programs
        targeting, 110, 111, 116
    hiring tests for, 106–107
    in management, 103, 106, 107, 109
    mentoring programs for, 110–111
    performance reviews and,
        107–108
modesty, 9, 26, 54, 70, 72
Moore, Roy, 123, 124–125

Morgan Stanley, 103
mothers, 3, 14, 19, 32, 145, 148, 172
motivation, 23–24
multinational companies, 146, 152, 154, 155

narcissists, 24
negative incentives, 105
networks/networking, 18, 33
    in emerging markets, 152–153
    informal, 14–15
    lack of access to, 45
    leveraging, 55
    "old girls," 161, 177
    outside of company, 154–155
    peer, 171
    programs, 177
    role of, 177
    socializing and, 128–129
Nixon, Richard, 2
Nohria, Dean Nitin, 190–191
nonlinear career paths, 166–167
nonverbal dominance, 9

Obama, Barack, 62
objectivity, in performance
    evaluation, 4, 16, 107–108
Obodaru, Otilia, 51–66
off-ramping, 157–178
    ambition and, 168–169
    penalties of, 164–166, 167
    reasons for, 157–162, 165, 175–176
    returning to workforce after, 5, 19, 159, 162–164, 175–176
    statistics on, 158–159, 163
"old girls" networks, 161, 177
on-ramping, 5, 19, 159, 162–164, 175–178
opt-out revolution, 157–158
    See also off-ramping
organizational culture
    employee survey on, 134–137
    of exclusion, 101

sexism in, 91–102
sexual harassment and, 119–130
stigmatization of flexible work
    arrangements in, 174–175
overseas assignments, 154

parental leave, 19, 186
parental responsibilities. See family
    demands
participative leadership, 13
part-time employment, 160–161, 164, 166–167, 169, 172
peer networking, 171
PepsiCo, 157
performance evaluation
    based on productivity, 4, 16
    bias in, 107–108
    criteria for, 4, 16
    for promotions, 67
    teams and, 75
performance feedback, 47–48, 51, 53, 59, 60
Pfizer, 155, 172
Piaget, Jean, 23
power dynamics, 74, 140
prejudice, 4, 5–7, 16
Price, Roy, 128
productivity, 4, 16
professional identities, 163–164
promotions
    gender gap in, 5, 6–7, 9
    performance ratings and, 107–108
    preparation for, 18
    race and, 6–7
    social accountability and, 114, 115
    time needed for, 18–19
publicly traded companies, women
    represented in, 1
public sector jobs, 149
purpose, sense of, 41–42, 48–50

questions, asking, 70, 76–77

race, promotions and, 6–7
racial discrimination, 106, 111,
    113–114
rape, 151
    See also sexual harassment
rapport, 74
Rashid, Ripa, 145–155
Reardon, Kathleen, 91–102
recognition
    for accomplishments, 83
    ambition and, 24–25, 168
    deferring of, 25–29
    femininity and, 30
    forfeiting opportunities for, 34–35
    gender differences in, 26–27
    lack of, for women, 26–27
    structures of, 32–33
recruitment tools, 5, 16–17, 110, 111
reduced-hour jobs, 160, 169, 172
reentry, to workforce, 5, 19, 159,
    162–164, 175–176
referrals, 4–5, 16–17
Ridgeway, Cecilia, 11
ritual opposition, 81–82
role models
    lack of female, 44
    for visioning, 55
Russia, 150, 151

safety, 119, 131, 136, 150–151
Sandberg, Sheryl, 179–191
Sayers, Dorothy, 37
second-generation gender bias,
    42–46, 50
self-confidence, 40, 45, 55, 67–68
self-deprecation, 25–29
self-employment, 164
self-managed teams, 112–113, 116
self-promotion, 9, 64–65, 74–75
sex discrimination claims, 103
sexism, speaking up about, 91–102
sexual assault. *See* rape; sexual ha-
    rassment

sexual harassment
    #MeToo movement and, 120–122,
        125, 137
    behaviors in, 139
    changes in attitudes toward,
        119–130
    credibility of complaints of, 126
    employee survey on, 130–137
    firings and, 125–127
    frequency of, 141
    in hospitality industry, 119
    impacts of, 120, 123
    in legal profession, 120–121
    men and, 119–120, 122, 127, 128
    pervasiveness of, 120–121
    policies, 127
    power dynamics and, 140
    prevalence of, 138–144
    settlement of complaints of,
        125–127
    spectrum of, 130
    survey on, 134–144
    underreporting of, 142–143
sexual identity, 29–30, 37
Siemens, 152
Silicon Valley, 104
"slut shaming," 120, 124
Smith Barney, 103
social accountability, 104, 113–115
social capital
    building, 5, 17–18
    underinvestment in, 14–15
social change, 11
social networks, 4–5, 16–17
social pressures, 37
Sorvino, Mira, 122
sponsorship programs, 45,
    186–187
    See also mentoring programs
spouses' income, 161–162, 163
status, giving criticism and, 83–84
stay-at-home parents, 181–182
Steinem, Gloria, 100–102

stereotypes
    biblical, 124
    conforming to, 188
    gender, 2, 17, 44, 46, 47, 49, 55, 64
    masculine, 128
    Vengeful Lying Slut, 120, 121, 124
stigma, of flexible work
    arrangements, 174-175
Stouffer, Samuel, 112
stress, 36-37
Strober, Myra H., 98-100
Summers, Larry, 187

talent
    college recruitment of, 110-113,
        116-117, 151-152
    demand for, 177
    in emerging markets, 145-155
    international assignments for, 154
    retaining female, 177-178
    shortage of, 146, 159
Tannen, Deborah, 9, 67-89
teams
    performance evaluation and, 75
    self-managed, 112-113, 116
    sole female member of, 5, 17
telecommuting, 161, 167
Thatcher, Margaret, 64
Thomas, Clarence, 124
Thomas, R. Roosevelt, Jr., 106
360-degree feedback, 47, 51, 53,
    59, 60
Time's Up movement, 125
tokenism, 5, 17
top executives
    See also leaders/leadership
    critical mass of female, 5
    lack of female, 1-3
toxic masculinity, 127
transactional leadership, 12
transformational leadership, 12
turn taking, in communication,
    69-70

United Arab Emirates, 145, 149, 150
U.S. Government Accountability
    Office, 6
U.S. military, 111-112

Vengeful Lying Slut stereotype, 120,
    124
verbal intimidation, 9
verbal opposition, 71, 81-82
vision/visioning, 51-66
    communication of, 55
    importance of, 54, 65
    meaning of, 58, 63
    ratings on, 60
    skills, 54-55
    by women, 51-65

wages
    decreased, after time out of
        workforce, 164-166, 167
    gender gap in, 5-6
Weinstein, Harvey, 119, 120, 121, 122,
    126, 127, 137
Williams, Joan C., 119-130
women
    ambition of, 21-37, 147, 168-169,
        176-177
    barriers facing, 2-15, 20, 29-35,
        39-50, 169, 182-183
    business owners, 99
    college recruitment programs
        targeting, 117
    in emerging markets, 145-155
    experience of, as leaders, 181
    family demands on, 4, 13-14,
        32-33, 37, 148-149
    lack of, in top leadership, 1-3
    leadership style of, 3, 4, 10-13
    leaving workforce, 157-162
    likeability of, as leaders, 187-189
    linguistic style of, 72-73
    mentoring programs for, 110-111
    opportunities for, 35-36

perceptions about, 48–49
priorities of, 168
qualities associated with, 8–10
reentering workforce, 5, 19, 159, 162–164, 175–176
resistance to leadership of, 4, 7–10
self-deprecation by, 25–29
self-promotion and, 9, 64–65, 74–75
as sole member of team, 5, 17
stereotypes about, 2, 17, 44, 46, 47, 49, 55, 64, 120, 121, 124, 125
vision and, 51–65
Women at Intel Network (WIN), 153
workforce
returning to, 5, 19, 159, 162–164, 175–176
women leaving, 157–162, 164–166
work hours, 16, 153, 160, 167, 169, 172, 183–184

working mothers. *See* mothers
work/life balance, 167, 174–175, 183–184
work-life policies, 174–175
workplace
changes in, 119–130
climate survey, 134–137
discrimination, 34
hostile, 91–102, 119–123, 130–137
speaking up about sexism in, 91–102
sexual harassment in, 119–130, 137–144
workplace climate survey, 134–137
workplace culture. *See* organizational culture
work practices, 44–45, 46
work relationships, 128–130

Youth Development Study, 139

Invaluable insights
always at your fingertips

With an All-Access subscription to
Harvard Business Review, you'll get
so much more than a magazine.

Exclusive online content and tools
you can put to use today

My Library, your personal workspace for sharing,
saving, and organizing HBR.org articles and tools

Unlimited access to more than 4,000 articles in the
Harvard Business Review archive

Subscribe today at hbr.org/subnow

The most important management ideas all in one place.

We hope you enjoyed this book from *Harvard Business Review*. Now you can get even more with HBR's 10 Must Reads Boxed Set. From books on leadership and strategy to managing yourself and others, this 6-book collection delivers articles on the most essential business topics to help you succeed.

HBR's 10 Must Reads Series

The definitive collection of ideas and best practices on our most sought-after topics from the best minds in business.

- Change Management
- Collaboration
- Communication
- Emotional Intelligence
- Innovation
- Leadership
- Making Smart Decisions

- Managing Across Cultures
- Managing People
- Managing Yourself
- Strategic Marketing
- Strategy
- Teams
- The Essentials

hbr.org/mustreads

Buy for your team, clients, or event.
Visit hbr.org/bulksales for quantity discount rates.